John Talbot Dillon

Letters from an English Traveller in Spain in 1778

On the origin and progress of poetry in that kingdom

John Talbot Dillon

Letters from an English Traveller in Spain in 1778
On the origin and progress of poetry in that kingdom

ISBN/EAN: 9783743413382

Manufactured in Europe, USA, Canada, Australia, Japa

Cover: Foto ©ninafisch / pixelio.de

Manufactured and distributed by brebook publishing software (www.brebook.com)

John Talbot Dillon

Letters from an English Traveller in Spain in 1778

LETTERS

FROM AN

ENGLISH TRAVELLER

IN

SPAIN, IN 1778,

ON THE

ORIGIN and PROGRESS

OF

POETRY

IN THAT KINGDOM;

With occasional Reflections on MANNERS and CUSTOMS;
And ILLUSTRATIONS of the Romance of DON QUIXOTE.

ADORNED WITH

Portraits of the most eminent Poets.

Sed idem
Pacis eras, med. ufque belli. HOR.

LONDON;

Printed for R. BALDWIN, PATER NOSTER ROW;
And fold by PEARSON AND ROLLASON, BIRMINGHAM.
M. DCC LXXXI.

ERRATA.

Page 25, line 3, for *Gemblacemfis*, read *Gemblacenfis*.
52, line 3, for *Don Don*, read *Don*.
57, laft line of note for *Ovihuela*, read *Orihuela*.
87, laft line, for *Bracenfes* read *Bracharenfes*.
125, verfes, line 4, for *veres* read *veces*.
131, line 4th, of verfes, for *ninguno duo*, read *ninguno*.
134, line 14, for *fatyr*, read *fatire*.
159, line 16, for *Cetinia*, read *Cetina*.
166, laft line for *winquefort* read *wiquefort*.
270, line 14, for *Elvina*, read *Elvira*.
288, line 1ft, for *not only*, read *fhe not only*.

Directions for the Plates.

Plate 1ft, Don Francifco de Quevedo, to face the title.
2nd, Garcilafo de la Vega, to face page 159.
3d, Don Alonfo de Ercilla, to face 222.
4th, Lope de Vega, to face 249.

PREFACE.

SO many English travellers have of late published their remarks in their respective tours
through Spain, that it is not without the utmost
deference that the present Letters are offered
to the public; as not only the most remarkable
objects in that kingdom have been fully described, but we have moreover had catalogues of
greek and latin books in libraries, lists of pictures, and circumstantial accounts of buildings,
both Roman, Gothic and Saracenie, annexed to
the various incidents of travelling.—Another
writer has had recourse to the very rocks and
mountains, has dug into the bowels of the
earth, and visited the mines, describing the
subterraneous kingdoms of nature, as well as
the various trees, and plants that cover the sur-
face of that extensive country. What then remains to the present writer? or how can he
flatter himself with presenting any new matter
worthy the attention of his readers, that will
stand the test, before the piercing eye of criti-
cism? yet methinks whatever may have been
the cause, whether from bad roads, wretched
inns, or extravagant price of provisions, in the
course of these different peregrinations; the
mountain of Parnassus has not been visited by the
curious traveller, and the spanish muse has tun-

A 2

ed

ed her lyre without being difturbed by the unhallowed ftep of the rambling ftranger.— Should this be the cafe, and that the author fhould have preferred the Caftalian fpring to the tempting juice of the La Mancha grape, he ftill claims indulgence for the many imperfections of the following fketch, while he truly dreads the charge of intoxication from thefe fhallow draughts!* at the fame time he acknowleges to have taken rather a curfory view of Don Quixote's library, and fome poems . are not mentioned fuch as the *Auftriada* of John Rufo, *The Tears of Angelica*, *The Fortune of Love* of Antonio Lofrafco of Sardinia, with fome others praifed by Cervantes. However tranfient, the merit of thefe may have been, it is not fo with an ingenious and burlefque poem intitled the *Mofchea* by Jofeph de Villaviciofa, which fhould not be forgotten, though not particularly mentioned in this work: the poet has defcribed with infinite humour and pleafantry the inconveniences arifing from that troublefome infect the mofchetto: a new edition of it was lately publifhed at Madrid and dedicated to our ambaffador then at that court, Lord Grantham, evidently

* See Pope's Effay on Criticifm.

manifefting

manifesting in the person of that accomplished nobleman, a sensibility of the impartial and refined Judgment of the British nation, of which the spanish muse seemed desirous to court the particular favour and applause.

It has been said by a great and learned french writer " that the Spaniards have but one book, and that one, shews the ridicule of all the others." How far such a general reflection appears strained and tinctured with national prejudice, I shall leave to others to consider : --- wishing to reverse so severe a sentence, I now stand before the court of Apollo, and petition for a hearing. Can we avoid doing that justice to the surprising genius of Lope de Vega, the contemporary, and in a manner rival, of our immortal Shakespeare; or can we refuse encomiums to the learned and unfortunate Quevedo? to whom we may fairly apply the lines of Pope in favour of one of our own poets.

To him the wit of Greece and Rome was known,
And ev'ry author's merit but his own.

To those who may be pleased with poetical numbers, a few specimens are added of the different kinds of Spanish versification. With respect to the judgement passed on the several

poets,

poets, I have followed the opinions of their own countrymen, and I further acknowledge my particular obligations for this purpofe, to two Spanifh academicians, Don Lewis Jofeph Velazquez, Knt. of the order of St. James, in his Effay on Spanifh poetry; and to the new Spanifh Parnaffus, of Don John Jofeph Lopez de Sedano, Knt of the order of Carlos Tercero; as well as to the pofthumous Memoirs intended for the hiftory of poetry and Spanifh poets, by the late father Sarmiento, a learned Benedictine, from whofe valuable writings I have felected much information: ftill the field is fo ample that a great deal remains unexplored : I have in a manner only traced the fkeleton of a gigantic figure, whofe proportions, like the Farnefian hercules, are more eafily admired, than defcribed. If therefore from want of abilities equal to the fubject, I am deficient; I fhall think myfelf amply rewarded, if on the whole, it may not be thought, I have already faid too much, and that I do not fall under the imputation mentioned by Swift of fome writers, when he fays, " The moft accomplifhed way of ufing books at prefent is, to ferve them as fome do lords, learn their titles, and then brag of their acquaintance."

T A B L E

O F

C O N T E N T S.

LETTER

viii CONTENTS.

LETTER

LETTER

LETTER XV.

LETTER XVI.

LETTER XVII.

LETTER XVIII.

LETTER XIX.

LETTERS

ON THE

ORIGIN

OF

SPANISH POETRY.

LETTER I.

*Voyage to Barcelona.—College of Trobadours.—
Castilian language described.*

DEAR SIR,

BARCELONA, 2d MAY, 1778.

WHEN I took my leave of you at Genoa, and embarked in an English veſſel for Barcelona, I left you reading Petrarch. You may recollect I informed you how much that illuſtrious poet had con-tributed to poliſh and improve the Poetry of Spain, where he had nu-merous admirers, as well as imita-

B   tors,

tors, who introduced his metre into
their language, though not without
oppofition at firft, from national prejudice.

You acquainted me that you had
already begun to read Don Quixote
in its original language, and the celebrated Spanifh tranflation of the
Aminta of Taffo, by Jauregui, found
in Don Quixote's library, and fo
highly praifed by Cervantes. You
requefted my opinion concerning the
Poetry of Spain, with fome information relating to their Poets, the time
when they flourifhed, and where their
works were printed. Senfible how
unequal I am to the tafk, I promifed
however to give you in the courfe of
my tour, a flight fketch of the Origin and Progrefs of national Poetry

in

in that kingdom, to trace its viciſſitudes through the mazes of hiſtory and conqueſt, after the irruption of the northern hive, and ſucceeding invaſion of the Saracens; finally, its improvement from the Trobadours, as well as flouriſhing ſtate under the kings of Caſtile: particularly after they had driven out the Moors and diſcovered a new world, furniſhing additional ſcenes to the fancy of the poet, and unexplored regions to the elegant pen of the hiſtorian.

I arrived at this famous city after a pleaſant paſſage of ſeven days. Our veſſel was filled with a motley collection of paſſengers, conſiſting of Spaniſh tumblers returning to Valencia, Italian actreſſes and fidlers, recruit-

ing

ing serjeants, pilgrims, and friars. As the weather was fine, we were continually entertained upon deck with the shrill fife of the soldier, the jarring sound of a dissonant guitarre, the din of the castanets, with the *fandango* dance, and the love songs of the actresses; all which were occasionally interrupted by the grave discourse of a venerable friar, who had lived many years at Rome, and was now returning home wrapt up in monastic forms and regulations.— We had some blowing weather in crossing the gulph of Lyons, that gave a pause to our mirth; but the sea became smooth like glass, as we drew near to Barcelona, when the pleasing sight of the coast, with the verdant hills in the blooming May,

enraptured

enraptured the eye, while the fanning breezes wafted us forward, and our chearful companions made this little voyage the moſt pleaſant I had ever performed; thus we entered the harbour in triumph, amidſt the exultations of our jolly bacchanalians, who made the hills echo with their vociferation.

So much for muſic. Let me now return to the poets, for I am already on claſſic ground, and the ſeat of the muſes. It was in this city that a college was firſt founded for the Trobadours, who were ſettled here towards the end of the fourteenth century, by John the ıſt king of Aragon, who ſent a ſolemn embaſſy to France for the purpoſe, deſiring aſſiſtance from the fociety of Trobadours at Thouloufe, in order to introduce the *Gaya Sciencia* into Spain, a requeft which was immediately granted; and two principal perfons were fent to Barcelona, where they formed an eftablifhment: but before I take up the Poets, I muft fay a few words concerning the language, as the groundwork on which this fuperftructure. was to be raifed.

The common language of Spain is called *Caftilian*, or *Romance*. This is what is printed in books, and fpoken at court, and in the univerfities. The city of Toledo was confidered the ftandard, when the refidence of the monarchs; but now Madrid undoubtedly bears the palm. This

is

is the language that prevails in the two Caſtiles, Leon, Aragon, Eſtremadura, Andaluſia, Navarre, Rioja and the mountains of Burgos; in all which places it is common, with more or leſs purity, attended with an accent called *Tonillo*, but without any variety of dialect. It is not ſo in Aſturias, Galicia, Valencia and Catalonia, where they have a provincial dialect, inſomuch that the Caſtilian language is not univerſal, though generally well underſtood, and written in all parts, except in the mountains of Navarre and Biſcay, where it is neither ſpoken, written, nor underſtood by the common people, who have a different language of their own, unconnected with the Caſtilian; but this is not

B 4

the

the cafe in Catalonia, Valencia, and Galicia, the dialects of which are corruptions of the latin as well as the Caftilian; of courfe the affinity of the latter has been clofer, and its progrefs more extenfive.

From fuch a diverfity of dialects it is natural to fuppofe that no modern language abounds more than the Spanifh with foreign expreffions, owing to the variety of nations that have vifited that kingdom, conquered it, or become fubject to its dominion; which makes it difficult to trace the origin of its words, and has fwelled the dictionary of the Spanifh academy to fix volumes in folio, which is yet thought fo deficient, that the firft volume has been reprinted with con-

fiderable

siderable additions, for whoever attempts an etymological work of this nature, muft, exclufive of modern languages, poffefs a rich fund of oriental literature, added to a perfect knowledge of latin and greek, a judgment of which may be formed from the fpecimen exhibited by the learned Cobarruvias (a). If then we fuppofe the Spanifh language to be divided into 100 parts, fixty muft be allotted to latin, ten to greek, ten to the goths and northern nations, ten hebrew and arabic, and ten german, italian, and french, with the new words imported from the Eaft and Weft-Indies.

(a) Teforo de la lengua Caftellana o Efpanola, por Don Sebaftian de Cobarruvias Orozco. Madrid, 1611.

In

In the year 1300 there were five national languages fpoken in Spain, viz, the Caftilian, Lemofin, Portuguefe, Galician, and Bifcayan, in their refpective provinces; while the following dead languages were equally common, viz, the hebrew amongft the Jews, the arabic amongft the Mahometans, and the latin and greek amongft the Chriftians. Aldrete has fairly proved in his book on the "Origin of the Caftilian language," that it never exifted as a diftinct language prior to the invafion of the goths, and that it owed its origin to a corruption from the latin, though the exact time could not be fixed. Several parchment infcriptions and poems having been difcovered and dug up in Granada in the fixteenth century, weakly attributed to St. Cecilius

a dif-

a difciple of St. James, and fuppofed
to be coeval with the days of the a-
poftles; yet written in the Spanifh
language; thefe were alleged with an
intemperate zeal againft Aldrete,
who, dreading the iron hand of fu-
perftition, and not daring to contra-
dict the blind notions of his countrymen, unwilling at the fame time to
give up his opinion, he fell upon this
fingular device, " that thefe writings
were delivered in a prophetic ftrain,"
and thus avoided the conteft. Thefe
monuments of grofs and bigoted cre-
dulity were carefully fent to Rome to
be examined, where they have fince
been finally condemned, and the bu-
finefs is now at an end (a). We need

(a) Papebrochius, in his Life of Ferdinand the
faint, for the 30th of May, has given a full account
of thefe Granada poems; even the reading of them

not.

not then be furprifed at their ignorance in other matters relating to the
antiquities and hiftory of their country. Father Sarmiento, a learned benedictine, complains, that there are
feveral hebrew and arabic books, relating to Spain, with which his own
countrymen are totally unacquainted ; adding that *Albupharage* was
tranflated by an Englifhman, *Elmacin*
by a Dutchman, and the *Geographia
Nubienfis* by a Maronite, being all a-
rabic compofitions, which, without
abfolutely belonging to Spanifh hiftory, are replete with a variety of matter that greatly ferves to illuftrate
its hiftory and geography. But let

was prohibited in 1641, and they were finally con-
_____ in 1682. "Memorias para la hiftoria de la
_____ octas Efpanoles. Por El Rmo. P. M,
_____ _____ nto. Madrid, 1775."

me

me not involve you in such a chaos. I
have already exercifed your patience
and let me rather entertain you with
this agreeable climate, fo particularly inviting at this feafon of the
year.

I have made an excurfion to the
famous mountain of Montferrat, the
wonder of naturalifts, which our englifh travellers in Spain have fufficiently defcribed. I fpeak of it only in a poetical ftyle, as it has been
celebrated in heroic verfe by Chrifto-
pher de Virues of Valencia, whofe
poem of *Monferrate* I fend you herewith, which makes it unneceffary for
me to add any more on the fubject.
You may remember this poem was
alfo in Don Quixote's library, and
preferved

preferved from the flames. Should
this find you reading that incompara-
ble romance, obferve that I have juft
been on the fpot near the walls of
this city, where the Bachelor Sanfon
Carrafco, alias the intrepid *Caballero
de la Blanca Luna*, overthrew in fingle
combat the unfortunate hero of *La
Mancha*, and gave the finifhing ftroke
to his extravagant adventures.

Adieu.

LETTER II.

Latin poets in Spain after the conquest of the Romans, and under the Goths.

BARCELONA, 12th MAY, 1778.

AS you proposed to set out immediately for England, and to pass with the utmost expedition through France, I hope I shall soon hear of your safe arrival, as it will be some time before I can join you. Whatever may be the novelties and pleasure arising from travel, the mind naturally preponderates towards home, and I seldom pass a day without casting a wistful eye towards England, and enjoying, in private,

the

the pleafing expectation of returning to my own country, and once more with rapture, to hail fair Britannia!

I find, fince I came here, that I had a narrow efcape, and that if I had been longer at fea, and obliged by any accident, to put into Marfeilles, our fhip would have been feized and ourfelves become the dupes of a perfidious and inveterate enemy! but thank God we have had the good fortune to avoid their deceitful wiles.

Having mentioned to you the defeat of the hero of *La Mancha*, you will perhaps expect from this place a fcene on the gallies, fimilar to the one defcribed in fo lively a manner in Don Quixote, but thofe days

are

are paſt at Barcelona; the harbour has long ſince been choaked up with ſand; the plans offered to remedy this defect have been rejected, and though the city and port have lately been beautified, this place is only frequented by ſmall veſſels, and the arſenal which ſerved for thoſe gallies, formerly the terror of the Moors, is now converted into a foundery of cannon, where I have ſeen them buſy at work. The corſairs are well apprized of this alteration, for the day I entered Barcelona, I ſaw two of their cruiſers ſtand cloſe in to the mouth of the harbour, with an exulting indifference.

I have ſpent my time very agreeably in this place, and have been of ſe-

veral

veral chearful parties in the neighbourhood. I have laid in a provifion of good *Mataro* wine, which is a red wine little inferior to *Port*, and confiderably cheaper, and have had the pleafure to drink your health in a bumper of excellent *Sitges*, by far the beft of all the Catalonian wines, which in general have a roughnefs, with a certain *gout de terroir*.

Previous to my departure for Valencia, I refume my favourite fubject, and entertain you with the poets after the conqueft of the Romans, and under the Goths, as introductory to what I fhall fay of the Caftilian mufe when I come to illuftrate its different eras, under its monarchs, till the fucceffion of a

french

french prince to the throne of Spain. I shall point out the various *Cancioneros*, or collections, that have been made of the Poets, the Spanish translations of the greek and latin classics, and italian poets, as well as the Spanish writers who have professionally treated of the art.

We read that the natives were fond of poetry time immemorial, and cultivated it with singular. delight. Silius Italicus relates, that the people of Galicia composed and sung verses in their original tongue. Strabo extols the ingenuity of the *Turdetani*, and says that they had histories and poems, as well as laws written in verse, when it was first applied, as Horace says, to soften the manners,

and

and introduce order and decorum into civil society. As to the primitive language of Spain we are still in the dark concerning it, if we give it a greek or phœnician original, a similar genius of poetry will naturally follow; if it should be compared to the hebrew, which neither you nor I understand, I must refer you to a learned british prelate, to whose refined and classical taste we are indebted for a just idea of the poetry of that people.

After Spain had been conquered by the Romans, it insensibly became the seat of the muses. Caius Julius Hyginus, the freedman of Augustus, and according to Suetonius, a Spaniard by birth, was the intimate friend of Ovid, and is said to be the author of

the

the aftronomical poetry that goes under his name. In the fame age flourished Sextilius Hena, of whom Seneca fpeaks but indifferently, taxing him with being more ingenious than learned, and fo flighty and unequal withal, that he feemed to fall into the bombaft and fuftian which Cicero takes notice of in the poets of Cordova, who perhaps had a peculiarity of manner and diction, fuch as even Livy the hiftorian could not diveft himfelf of. The city of Cordova produced three good poets under that monfter Nero, the two Senecas and Lucan. The tragedies of Seneca are the only latin ones extant of the ancients. Martial of Bilbilis, now Bambola in Aragon, lived under Domitian. He mentions feveral

other

other poets that made a figure in his
days; such as Unicus, his kinsman,
whose brother was also a poet, Cani-
us of Cadiz, Decianus of Merida, and
Licianus also of Bilbilis.   From this
time down to the emperor Constan-
tine, the poetic vein seems to have
greatly declined.   Juvencus, a priest,
put the gospel into hexameter verse,
and was the first ecclesiastical bard.
Arator translated the acts of the apos-
tles into hexameters, and was followed by Sedulius.   Latinus Pacatus, in
a panegyric on the emperor Theodo-
sius, declares, that Spain abounded
in valiant soldiers, eloquent orators,
and excellent poets.   St. Jerome
speaks of Aquilius Severus, a Spanish
poet, who flourished under Valenti-
nian.   Prudentius, who lived in the

fourth

fourth century, is equally read for the harmony of his numbers, as for the information he gives of the church hiſtory of his time.

We now come to the fifth century, when the ſavage goth overrun the dominions of Spain; though we muſt not charge theſe invaders with the ignorance and barbarity of the age, or make them the only deſ-poilers of that taſte which the ro-mans had left with the Spaniards. A more powerful cauſe operated on the mind: The gloom of ſuperſtition univerſally prevailed, the eccleſiaſ-tic poet full of holy zeal for religion, was afraid to break in on its myſte-ries, and his genius was cramped; without a ſpark of poetic fire he writ

C 4

hymns

hymns for the church, to ſtrengthen the devotion of the people, who were cautioned againſt the allegory of the gentiles ; ſo that by degrees every idea of the ſublime and beautiful was loſt. Idacius however ſpeaks of a Spaniſh poet called Marobaudes, who was of illuſtrious birth, and an excellent orator, worthy to be claſſed with the ancients ; adding that he flouriſhed under Theodoſius the 2nd, in whoſe days alſo lived Dracontius, who according to Iſidore writ an heroic poem on the creation of the world.

In the fifth century we find the biſhop Ciponius, who compoſed a poem in which he compares the ſtory of Phaeton to the fallen angels ; a ſingular alluſion for a chriſtian prelate.

In

In the sixth century flourished Orencius, who is spoken of by Segebert Gemblacemcis, and writ a poem entitled *Commonitorium,* in hexameters and pentameters, published with notes by father Martin Antonio del Rio, and more correctly by Don Juan Tamayo de Salazar. In the seventh century we have St. Ildefonsus, archbishop of Toledo, who composed epigrams and epitaphs. St. Eugenius, archbishop of the same church, continued the poem of Dracontius on the creation of the world; a lofty theme! seemingly reserved for the dignity of our own language, as the experience of many ages has evidently shewn, that it belonged to the divine Milton alone, to treat so sublime a subject, and sing

 " Of man's first disobedience."

LETTER III.

*Journey to Valencia. Latin Poetry under the
Saracens. Library of Don Gregorio Mayans.*

VALENCIA, 22nd MAY, 1778.

THE badnefs of roads, the
want of poft-horfes and car-
riages with the inconvenience of mi-
ferable inns, are common topics for
travellers in this country; but we muft
attribute it rather to their gothic laws
and bad policy of government, than
to the natural difpofition of the people. 'Till the old tenures are abolifhed, as well as the variety of fhack-
les with which induftry is fettered,
the traveller muft bear every thing

with

with patience; for otherwife, he only offers an idle and ufelefs complaint! In every town and village
the privilege of keeping an inn be-
longs to the lord of the manor or the
corporation. If a private perfon without authority was to make the attempt he would incur a fevere penal-
ty, and be immediately punifhed.
Thus the privileged innholder fleeces
the paffenger with impunity, that he
may pay an exorbitant rent to the land-
lord, befides a confiderable premium
at entrance. In many places this
occupation is deemed a public office,
which every one in his turn is obliged
to difcharge, fometimes for a term of
three years. When the lot happens
to fall on an indigent peafant, what
comfort can be found under his
roof?

roof? How can fuch an inn be provided with furniture, and what fort
of beds are to be expected from a
man, who wrapped up in his cloak
has flept all his life on the ground?
But this is not all: provifions are a-
nother monopoly. It would be highly criminal for an inn-keeper to have
a larder, or even wine in his cellar;
every thing muft be purchafed at appointed places, where the wearied
traveller muft go or fend his fervants,
and even then feldom finds what he
wants; at thefe places, difdain and
fcorn is the leaft he is to expect, added
to the reception of an enemy rather
than a friend, and he curfes the land-
lord, his houfe, and his country; for
which reafon the natives, who know
what they have to expect, feldom ftir

from

from home, unlefs urged by the utmoft neceffity; by which means the country is unhofpitable, and the traveller as much at a lofs as in the defarts of Arabia.

Under thefe forbidding circum-ftances, animated by that infatiable paffion, curiofity, I hired a carriage at Barcelona, drawn by mules, hav-ing previoufly provided myfelf with a kettle, knife, fork, and fpoon, napkins, and a little ftock of coffee, chocolate, tea, fugar, &c. with a camp-bed, and other field equipage; thus I fallied forth in queft of adven-tures, having obtained a permit from the Captain-general of the province to travel with fire-arms, which was inferted in my paffport, and in this manner,

manner, travelling at the rate of about twenty miles a day, I arrived happily at this pleafant city, delightfully fituated near the fea, in a beautiful vale, fo highly efteemed by the Moors, that they fondly conceived paradife to be feated in that part of heaven which hangs over it. No wonder then if the poetic vein fhould partake of the happy influence of the climate, and the Valencian mufe be fo remarkably infpired.

In my laft letter I am afraid I overpowered you with dulnefs, in wandering through the dark ages of gothic barbarity and ignorance; we now draw near to a more brilliant epocha, the invafion of Spain by the Saracens in the eighth century; which

brought

brought about a further revolution in the underſtanding of men, as well as in dominion ; ſince with the arts and ſciences, the Arabs introduced a new ſtrain of imagery to enliven the fancy of the poet; the muſe partook of its bold metaphor and lofty flight, robed in the ſplendid garb of fiction, decked with oriental pearl, and heightened with all the powers of imagination! Without tracing the remote origin of poetry from the ſongs of the gothic bards or the iſlandic ſcalds, the poetical field becomes animated, and the Rhunic enchantments feeble and dim, when compared with the boundleſs luxuriance of the Eaſt: however, we muſt not loſe ſight of the latin muſe, when in queſt of her Caſtilian deſcendant, but once more

behold

behold her with her difhevelled
locks, difguifed under gothic drape-
ry. Amongft thefe was Theodolphus,
bifhop of Orleans, in the eighth century, though a native of Spain, whofe
poems have been publifhed in France
by father Sirmond : thofe of Alvaro
of Cordova, in the ninth century,
and of Ciprian, arch-prieft of Cordova, have been preferved in Spain
by the late father Florez, a learned
monk and celebrated antiquary.—
Were it neceffary, I could foon fwell
the lift, for at that time poetry feemed to inflame every breaft. Alvaro of
Cordova particularly fpeaks of it, as
a vain amufement and paftime, in
which St. Eulogius and himfelf had
wafted much of their youth. It is from
thefe writers, and the imperceptible

decay

decay of the latin tongue, that we muſt trace the firſt dawn of the Caſtilian muſe; concerning which I mean to entertain you, when I have ranged a little further in this delightful ſpot, and beheld the variety of landſcapes, with which the bounteous hand of nature has every where enriched this charming and beautiful country.

In the courſe of my rambles amidſt orange groves, immenſe plantations of mulberry trees, and various pleaſant gardens, I have in vain ſought for the *Olivera de Valencia*, mentioned in Don Quixote. That famous and venerable tree, celebrated by floral games and rural ſports, now exiſts no more, though the olive is cul-

D tivated

tivated with the greateſt aſſiduity and yields excellent oil. Hearing that there was a veſſel in the road of Valencia, bound for England, I have ſent you a jar of oil; and ſome excellent olives, which though perhaps not ſo luſcious as thoſe from Andaluſia, that Cicero was ſo fond of; yet I hope may ſtill find a place at your table. The culture of the olive is general in all this part of the country. The method of propagating it, is ſtill the ſame as mentioned by Virgil:

" Quin & caudicibus ſectis mirabile dictu
" Truditur e ſicco radix oleagina ligno."

GEORG. 2. V. 30.

I have had the pleaſure to become acquainted with the learned and courteous Don Gregorio Mayans, former-

ly

ly librarian to the king; who now lives here, having a good eftate in this country, and to his politenefs I am much indebted for many civilities, as well as great information. To give you an account of his numerous writings in almoft every branch of literature and jurifprudence, would fill a volume. You have read his life of Cervantes, annexed to the Carteret edition of Don Quixote. He is now writing the life of Virgil, and is poffeffed of a moft curious and valuable library, chiefly of the writers of his own country, with many fcarce manufcripts, and a numerous collection of the old Spanifh tranflations of the greek and latin claffics. He is now in a very advanced age; but ftill preferves vivacity and a moft af-

fable

fable difpofition, added to a furprifing application. During the intrigues of the jefuits, who were afraid
of him, his houfe and library were
invefted by an armed force; dragoons
broke into his ftudy, and took away
many of his books by authority!---
Oh, happy England! where the property of individuals is facred, and
where the leaft violation of liberty,
meets with a fpirited and juft refentment from the people; of which we
have lately had fo ftriking an inftance
in a cafe of this nature. Such is the
public fpirit of our country, that if
the moft flagitious character is attacked either in his perfon or freedom---
I fay, were even fuch, ever to be
oppreffed, the tutelary genius of liberty guards the injured party with

her

her ſhield, in hopes that a due ſenſe of her protection, may correct the heart and reform paſt errors;---but Don Gregorio Mayans is juſt at my door, and I muſt bid you farewell.

LETTER

LETTER IV.

Attachment of the Spaniards to the Arabic numbers. Literature of the Spanish Jews.

VALENCIA 28th MAY 1778.

AS I postpone making you acquainted with the Castilian muse till my arrival at Madrid, I cannot refrain from troubling you with some further reflections on the saracens, tending to elucidate the influence which their government had over poetic numbers. The very faces of the present inhabitants carry such a striking resemblance of their ancestors, and the african cast of feature is

fo

fo perceptible, that I am infenfibly led into this fubject.

It being common for the vanquifh-ed to receive laws from the conque-ror, it was natural that Spain fhould fhare the fate of arms, and receive with the faracen yoke their manners and cuftoms. Thefe people having held a long poffeffion of this country, in-troduced their language, religion, and literature. The oriental ftyle of poetry pervaded every mind, and the exuberant genius of its compofition not only became univerfal, but in a manner worked the downfal of the roman numbers. Alvaro of Cordo-va, complains that the Spaniards had fo totally forgotten the latin tongue, and given the preference to arabic,

D 4

that

that it was difficult even amongſt a
thouſand people, to find one who
could write a latin letter. So great
was the attachment of the people to
the chaldaic books, and the literature
of the orientals, that they could write
arabic with remarkable purity, and
compoſe verſes with as much fluency
and elegance as the arabians themſelves. Not only charmed with their
poetry, they even embraced their religion; for Iſen, king of Cordova, who
died in 795, had three thouſand apoſ-
tates from chriſtianity, in his train.

Thus after a long period of near
eight hundred years that the dominion of the arabs continued; the provinces of Spain ſplit into numerous
dynaſties, flouriſhed in oriental literature

rature; whilſt the Caſtilians diſtinguiſhed themſelves in feats of arms,
and were ſpilling their blood in defence of their territories ; honour and
love were ſung by the bards, and
the arabic muſe furniſhed a numerous liſt of poets, whoſe names are
recorded in the *Bibliotheca Hiſpana* of
Don Nicolas Antonio ; the oriental
dictionary of Herbelot, and the arabic hiſpanic collection of manuſcripts
in the eſcurial, lately publiſhed at
Madrid, by Caſiri, a Maronite, in
two volumes in folio, at his catholic
majeſty's expence ; where a numerous
collection of poets may be found,
hitherto unnoticed, all which are
carefully preſerved in the valuable
library of the eſcurial. In this claſs
the province of Andaluſia particular

ly

ly. diftinguifhed itfelf; its inhabitants feemed animated with a peculiar brilliancy of compofition. The two academies of Cordova and Seville fhone beyond others. Their writers introduced harmony and numbers into the moft ferious fubjects, leaving nothing either in religion or politics, nor in any branch of polite arts which did not partake of their verfe and poetical enthufiafm. Ebn Tarhun of Seville who flourifhed in the year 691 of the hegira, raifed his mufe to the moft fublime themes; he fung of the creation of man; of the foul; and defcribed the temple of Mecca. Dhihaldin Alkazary who flourifhed in the fixth age of the hegira, writ a poem called " the treafure of poets"; while others employed themfelves in

comments

comments on their moſt claſſical writers.   Ebn Forgia, who lived in the
fifth age of the hegira, writ a commen-
tary on the famous poet Almotuabi,
and Ebn Macrana commented upon
the poem on animals by the perſian,
Abiotman.   Nor were the powers of
verſification confined to the men,
but extended equally to the fair ſex;
feveral ladies gave proofs of their talents, thofe of Andalufia in particular, did honour to the mufes, and
their works are preſerved in the efcurial; but none were more famous
than Maria Alphaifuli of Seville,
who was the Sappho of her time.

Befides thefe celebrated geniuffes,
the fame of many others has been
preferved in the dictionaries of arabic.

bic Spaniards, compiled by mahom⸗
etan writers ; fuch as the dictiona⸗
ry arabic and hifpanic, in the efcu⸗
rial, of all the caliphs, captains, phi⸗
lofophers, poets, and learned ladies
of Spain, in four large volumes, by
Ebn Alkhali Mahomed Ben Abdalla
in the year 710 of the hegira. Like⸗
wife the hiftory of all the Spaniards
and Africans, famous in arts and fci⸗
ences, particularly in poetry, writ⸗
ten by Ben Mahomed Abu Naffer
Alphath of Seville, who lived in the
fixth age of the hegira ; which book
is in the king of France's library.
Thus the arabic mufe flourifhed
while fupported by the cimeter,
and totally perifhed with its em⸗
pire, when the victorious arms of
Ferdinand and Ifabella drove the
moors out of Granada.

It

It is to thofe days we muft alfo look up, to form an idea of the literature of the Spanifh Jews, which was cherifhed by Mafters from Babylon, where they had academies fupported by themfelves; at a time when books were fo fcarce in Spain amongft chriftians, that in the beginning of the tenth century, one and the fame bible, with St Jerom's epiftles and other ecclefiaftical works ferved different monafteries. In the year 967, Rabbi Mofes and his fon Rabbi Enoch, having been taken by pirates, were fold as flaves at Cordova, and redeemed by their brethren, who eftablifhed a fchool at Cordova, of which Rabbi Mofes was appointed the head, who being defirous of returning back to his own country,

the

the moorish king of Cordova would not give his consent, rejoicing that his hebrew subjects had masters of their own religion at home, without the necessity of receiving them from a foreign university; and every indulgence was granted them with respect to their worship, exhibiting a true spirit of toleration, worthy to be followed by their christian successors.

In the year 1039, Rabbi Ezechias was put to death at Babylon, who had succeeded Hai Gazon, whose sons fled to Spain, by which the eldership of the Gaons became extinct, and their college was transferred to Cordova, from whence a swarm of hebrew poets issued forth, that have been noticed by various learned writers,

ters. Our countryman Thomas Hyde in his treatife *De ludis orientalibus,* mentions a hebrew poem on the game of chefs by Aben Ezra.

In Portugal, Rabbi David Ben Solomon Ben David Iachifa of Lifbon who lived in 1440, writ a treatife on hebrew poetry, which was tranflated into latin by Genebrard, and printed in 1587, at the end of his *Ifagoge,* to read hebrew without points; it abounds with quotations of the different metres of the hebrew poetry in Spain. They may be very fublime, but for my part I cannot read the language, either with points or without, and you will pardon this digreffion: however it gives us an idea of the flourifhing ftate of their
fchools

fchools in Cordova, Seville, Granada, and Toledo, and we need not be furprifed at the numerous hebrew proverbs, and modes of fpeech, that have crept into the caftilian language, and form a confpicuous part of its phrafeology; for though king John IId banifhed the Jews out of his kingdom, and the rigid and cruel inquifition was afterwards eftablifhed to purge the nation of that fect, yet all the horrors of that bloody tribunal, have not been able compleatly to effect this fanguinary purpofe.

The Spanifh language owes thefe people a particular obligation, for that curious verfion of the hebrew books of the old teftament, which long

long after their expulsion they first
printed at Ferrara, in 1553, in a go-
thic-spanish letter. A curious and
scarce book, comprehending many
energetic words, and peculiar expref-
sions, not to be found in the dictionary of the Spanish academy, and
which they seem to have cautiously a-
voided. This version is thought to
have been made by that learned
grammarian, David Kimchi, in the
tenth century. Father Sarmiento
has given many critical and judicious reasons for attributing this version to the age of Kimchi, and cen-
sures father Simon greatly, for faying it was made at the time it was
printed, when scarcely understood by
the Jews, *quam vix Judæi intelligunt.*
But you will say I am now going
on at an extravagant rate. Should

E   this

this find you safe returned, as I hope it will, remember me to my reverend friend, your brother; tell him what he lofes in not studying Spanish, and if he smiles at the conceit, remind him of Gafpar Lindenberg, who has written *de non contemnendis ex lingua hispanica utilitatibus theologicis* (a).

Having now furnished you sufficiently with hebrew, arabic, and gothic-fpanish information, and poured in upon you a legion of hard words, added to a variety of uncouth and harfh-founding names, I shall in my next touch upon the proceedings of the *Trobadours*, and then fet out for Madrid. Meanwhile I take my laft farewell of jews and mahometans.

(a) See Bibliotheca Græca, of Fabricius.

LETTER

LETTER V.

Proceedings of the Trobadours in the kingdom of Aragon, until its union to the crown of Castile. Character of the Marquis of Villena, an eminent poet.

VALENCIA, 31st MAY, 1778.

FROM the mistaken laws and notions concerning inns on the road, you will entertain a very indifferent idea of the interior police and government in towns in this country. Valencia, however, in this respect, deserves some exceptions, and I was not a little surprized at my return to my inn the second night after my arrival, to see the city guarded by a

patrol,

patrol, the men carrying lanthorns and poles in their hands like our London watchmen. This regulation is owing to the patriotic fpirit of Don Don Joachin Foz, a worthy magif-trate, who propofed it for the relief of a number of poor men, heretofore employed in the making of fire-works, a confiderable branch of in-duftry in this capital, till a late pro-clamation abolifhed them all over the kingdom. To find bread for a num-ber of diftreffed families, he hit up-on this laudable expedient. They walk the feveral ftreets from eleven at night, till five in the morning, cry-ing the hours and the weather, and keeping the peace as with us; but as this fine climate is feldom obfcured by dark nights or *cloudy mornings,* the ferene

atmofphere

atmofphere only affords them a mo-
notony of expreffion, and the word *fe-
reno*, becomes their conftant clamour;
from whence they have acquired the
name of *Sereneros*, which added to the
ftillnefs of the town, recalled to my
mind the beautiful night of Milton :

" Silence was pleafed; now glow'd the firmament
" With living fapphires: Hefperus that led
" The ftarry hoft rode brighteft." ——

I have now an opportunity of im-
proving myfelf in the poetry of the
Trobadours; for the language of this
country is a dialect of the provenzal;
and introduced itfelf with their verfe
in all thofe parts where their numbers prevailed; fuch as the coun-
ties of Languedoc, Rouffillon, and
Barcelona; kingdoms of Valencia,
Murcia, Majorca, Minorca, and Sar-

E 3

dinia;

dinia; where it remains to this day. The Spanish writers boast of their *Trobadours* as high as the twelfth or thirteenth centuries. William de Berguedam, a Catalan baron, was a *Trobadour,* and his poems are preserved in the vatican library, (*a*) as well as those of Nun de Mataplan (*b*); they also rank Raymond Lulli, of Majorca, in this class: but without looking so far back, I shall not go higher than the fourteenth century, when John the first, king of Aragon, who was also a poet, invited the *Trobadours* to settle in Barcelona, as we learn from Zurita, the learned and classic historian of that kingdom. The fifteenth century produced the celebrated Aufias March and James Roig, both of Valencia; the works of the former have been

(*a*) Codex 3204, 3205, and 3207.
(*b*) Codex 3204, and 3207.

turned

turned into Caſtilian verſe; the latter vented his ſpleen againſt women in a ſatyrical piece, called *Eſpil*, or " the Looking-glaſs," which ſeems to have been imitated by Prior. To court afterwards the favour of the fair ſex, Roig ſung the immaculate conception of the Virgin. This poet was phyſician to queen Mary of Aragon, wife to Alfonſo the fifth, and lived to be near a hundred years old. Though there are five editions of his works, none are later than 1562. The following lines may ſerve as a ſpecimen of his ſtyle :

> Noranta cinch
> O cent anys tinch
> Dels quals cinquanta
> O los ſexanta
> Del meus millors
> Penes dolors
> Man eſpletat.

E 4

In

In the fixteenth century, Peter Se-
raphi diftinguifhed himfelf in the Valencian dialect, and his poems are
prefixed to an edition of Aufias
March, printed at Barcelona, in 1560.
Many other bards are fpoken of,
though the exact period when they
lived cannot be afcertained. Among
the reft, Arnau Catalans (*a*), and Mo-
la (*b*), whofe works are in the vatican
library, Moffen Narias Vinyolles(*c*),
Vincent Ferradis, Don Franci de Ca-
ftelor, Miguel Perez, Juan de Verdancha and Moffen Bernardo Fenollar, of all whom, there are provenzal

(*a*) Codex 3205.

(*b*) —— 3207.

(*c*) The appellation of Moffen is peculiar to Valencia, in imitation of the French word *Monfieur*,
in the fame manner the Italians ftile a foreigner *Monfu*.

poems in the *Cancionero General* printed at Antwerp, in 1573. Fenollar was a native of Catalonia, and in that dialect, wrote in couplets, a poem on the "contemplation of Chrift" printed at Valencia, in 1493. They value themfelves greatly in this city on their early knowledge of the art of printing, when it was not in ufe in any other part of Spain; and fhew a latin dictionary, entitled, *Comprehenforium*(a), and a Salluft, printed in 1475: So that they foon followed

(a) The *Comprehenforium* has the following fentence at the end: " Præfens hujus comprehenforii præclarum opus Valentiæ impreffum, anno. m,cccc,lxxv. Die vero xxiii. menfis februarii finit feliciter."—The univerfity in the city of Valencia was founded in 1470, two other were afterwards founded in the fame province, viz. in the city of Gandia, in 1549, and at Ovibuela, in 1555.

the

the example of Oxford, where we find a book printed in 1468 (*a*), which was feveral years before Caxton practifed that art in England.

The provenzals generally made ufe of the hendecafyllable verfe : their poems confifted chiefly of fonnets, paftorals, and love fongs, which gave rife to a poetical tribunal, termed, *the court of love;* confifting of a felect number of eminent poets, who decided all controverfies amongft themfelves on thefe fubjects. The *Trobadours* were chiefly of the prime

(*a*) This book is in the public library at Cambridge. The title is, Expoficio Sancti Jeronimi in Simbolum Apoftolorum ad Papam Laurentium. At the end, Explicit expoficio, &c. Impreffa Oxonie & finita, an. dom. m,cccc,lxviii. —— See Hiftory and Art of Printing, by P. Luckombe, M. T. A. London, 1771.

nobility

nobility of the kingdom ; at length
they carried the poetic licence fo far,
as to give much fcandal to the public, and even to taint the reputation
of the palace, as well as of the ladies
of the court; for to make thefe entertainments more .fprightly, they 'invited minftrels, ftrollers, and buffoons,
which in fome meafure juftified the
precautions taken afterwards againft
them. However the kings of Aragon, Don John the 1ft, Don Martin,
and Don Ferdinand, reformed thefe
poetical confiftories, and ' brought
them into high reputation, in which
the laft mentioned fovereign was
greatly affifted by his kinfman, Don
Henry of Aragon, Marquis of Villena. Thefe monarchs affifted in perfon at their affemblies, where the
verfes

verſes of the candidates were recited, and the premiums diſtributed with all the magnificence and ſplendor of royalty. The poets who had gained the prizes were crowned with laurel, amidſt the acclamations of the ſpectators, added to the joyful ſound of muſical inſtruments, ſucceeded by an elegant repaſt: they were then conveyed home with a courtly attendance, and preſented with an excluſive privilege to ſing, and read their verſes in public at pleaſure: a noble inſtitution! the continuance of which was ſo ardently wiſhed for, by that immortal genius, Michael de Cervantes, the contemporary of Shakeſpear, and I will almoſt venture to add, in every reſpect his equal.

The

The mufes feem to have taken great delight in the kingdom of Aragon. At the coronation of king Alfonfo the fourth, in 1328, the Infant Don Pedro, earl of Ribagorza, and brother to the king, attended by the principal nobility, exhibited dances and a variety of paftorals, and fongs, compofed for that pleafing event. The *Joglar*, or poet Ramufet, fung a paftoral fong compofed by the earl; and Novelet, another *Joglar*, recited a poem of fix hundred verfes by the fame royal hand. The attachment to poetry feemed hereditary in the royal line of thefe princes, and continued in the Marquifs of Villena, who compofed the *Arte de la Gaya Sciencia*, for the ufe of the college of *Trobadours*, befides many other poems, which were

greatly

greatly admired, and frequently re-cited in public.

An hiftorical poem of all the poets of Aragon, has been fince compofed by Don John Francis Andres de Uftar-roz, hiftoriographer of Aragon, in imitation of that of the great Lope de Vega, of the poets of Caftile. Uftarroz compleated his in 1652, and thought firft to entitle it *Parnaffo Aragones*; but he altered his mind, and called it *Aganipe de Los Cifnes Aragonefes, celebrados in el clarin de la fama*: but it never was printed, and ftill remains in manufcript in the king's library at Madrid.

The union of the crown of Aragon with that of Caftile, in the perfon of king

king Ferdinand the fifth, who married Ifabella, heirefs of Caftile, feems to have eclipfed the fabling of the *Trobadours*. The Aragonians and Catalonians adopted the Caftilian dialect, when the influence of that kingdom prevailed, and the cultivation of its language and manners paved the way to honour and preferment. The poet Bofcan, of Barcelona, tuned his lyre to the genius of Caftile, and though a few bards attempted to fupport a languifhing mufe, Miguel Perez and juan de Verdancha, of Catalonia, introduced the Caftilian métre and rhyme into their verfe.—About this time Columbus difcovered a new world for the arms of Caftile, which gave fuch a fplendour to its court, and dignity to its language, that the Caftilian mufe fhone like a new conftellation

in

in the firmament! the wonderful exploits of intrepid heroes engroffed univerfal attention; the boundlefs love of fame immortalized the gallant foldier, while the fordid view of lucre difhonoured the adventurer, though it replenifhed the kingdom with gold. This unexpected event gave rife to a variety of paffions. The nation was roufed; the great empire of Montezuma ceafed in America; the Spanifh ftandard was difplayed in the new world; and the effeminate *Trobadours*, and their fongs, were entirely forgotten.

It remains for me, however, to fay fomething of the Marquis of Villena, whofe great character appears confpicuous in the poetical annals of his country;

country; being in a manner the father of poetry in Spain, as well as the brighteft ornament of his age. This illuftrious nobleman of the royal houfe of Aragon diftinguifhed himfelf early in poetry, philofophy, and aftrology, and with fuch attachment to this laft fcience, that amongft his ignorant countrymen he generally paffed for a necromancer. As his family had been difpoffeffed of the marquifate of Villena, Henry III. had given him the earldom of Cangas, and afterwards procured him to be elected grand mafter of the military and religious order of Calatrava. For this purpofe the marquis obtained a divorce from his wife under pretence of a natural impediment; then ceded the earldom of Cangas to the

F   crown,

crown that it might not fall into his order at his death, and was elected grand master: some of the knights however protested, and elected Don Luis de Gusman, a castilian nobleman; but the king went in person to Calatrava, put the marquis in possession, and every thing was quiet till the death of the king, when Guzman who had fled to Rome renewed his claim before the pope, and the knights refused further obedience. A long suit was commenced, which lasted six years, and was referred to a general chapter of the order of *Cister* held in Burgundy. Whilst this was depending, the marquis attended on his uncle Don Ferdinand of Aragon when he succeeded to that crown, and came with him to Barcelona,

where

where he prefided at the confiftory of *Trobadours*, and writ a theatrical piece, in which, juftice, truth, mercy, and peace, were the principal characters. In the midft of thefe rejoicings news came in 1414 that he had loft his election, and was deprived of his grandmafterfhip, with an injunction to cohabit again with his lawful wife, which he complied with, and became a fuitor at the court of king John II. then an infant, for an indemnification for his earldom of Cangas. After much folicitation he obtained the lordfhip of Iniefta, where he retired with his wife, and gave himfelf up to philofophy and the mufes. Befides a tranflation of Dante into profe, he tranflated the Æneis of Virgil in fpanifh verfe, at the

F 2

requeft .

requeſt of his kinſman John king of Navarre, and intended to dedicate it to that monarch, for which purpoſe he had affixed a painting, in which the king of Navarre is repreſented ſitting on his throne, and the marquis preſenting him his book; but when all this was compleated, he dropped his deſign, as that monarch went to war with the king of Caſtile, on which account he avoided all further communication with him. His moſt famous piece was his book on the *Gaya Sciencia*, which is a complete ſyſtem of poetry, rhetoric and oratory, beſides deſcribing all the ceremonies of the *Trobadours* at their public exhibitions. This work he dedicated to his illuſtrious and learned friend the marquis of Santillana.

After

After suffering much from the gout, he died in retirement in 1434; his fine library was burned under the notion of his knowledge of magic, and the bishop of Segovia, confessor to the king who was charged with this commission, is said to have reserved most of the books for himself.

Thus ended this great philosopher and friend of the muses, who was contemporary with our poet Lydgate, and had just reached the days of the renowned Chaucer, the father of english poetry, whom he greatly resembled. With him he ran the career of courts, and experienced the fickleness of royal favour, equally preferring retirement and study, and like him, had the merit of refining

the

the language and poetry of his country.   Thus the names of both bards
have been jointly handed down with
veneration, by a grateful pofterity!
If their verfe wanted melody, it was
owing to the inaccuracy of meafure,
and imperfection of language at
that time, when both the Englifh
and Caftilians feem more to have
courted the god Mars, than Apollo ;
for while the Caftilians were daily
encroaching on the Moors, the victorious banners of England were tri-
umphant in Paris, where our Henry
VI. was crowned king of France.

Alas, poor Macias! trufty efquire of
the grand mafter Villena, haplefs bard,
fhould I forget thee ! who didft fing
of love, and feel the fmart of its em-
bittered arrow: imprifoned for excefs

of

of paſſion, after the fair object of thy
love had been diſpoſed of; and had
given away her hand in thy abſence:
loaded with chains by Villena for the
follies of youth thou felleſt ſudden,
when bewailing thy fate; the Galician muſe ſtrewed flowers over thy
tomb, thy verſe is treaſured up in
the eſcurial, and the portugueſe bard
claims thee as a parent, for this was
thy ſong:

> Cativo de Mina triſtura
> Ja todos prenden eſpanto,
> E preguntan, que ventura
> Foy, que me atormenta tanto.
> Mas non ſe no mundo amigo,
> Que mais de meu quebranto
> Diga, deſto que vos digo
> Que ben ſee nunca devia,
> Al penſar que faz folia.

Cuyde

Cúyde fubir en alteza
Por cobrar mayor eftado,
E cay in tal pobreza,
Que moyro defemparado
Con pefar e con defefo
Que vos diray malfadado,
Loque yo he ben ovejo
Quando o loco cay mays alto
Sobir prende mayor falto.

LETTER

LETTER VI.

Journey from Valencia to Madrid—Battle of Almanza.—La Mancha.

MADRID, 12th JUNE, 1778.

I NOW date this from Madrid, where I arrived after a journey of nine days from Valencia, by the new road lately made from that city to this town, which is every-vhere marked out and rendered paſſable, though not compleated farther from Madrid than the town of *Ocana*, nine leagues from hence ; ſo far the road is excellent, and has mile ſtones ; but when the remainder will be finiſhed, or the intended canal of Caſtile, for

inland

inland navigation be compleated, no
one can tell; for while the family com-
pact has its fway, and they wafte
their treafures in fchemes of boundlefs ambition; they are only grafping
at a fhadow and impoverifhing their
people.   It is true, they have not as
yet taken off the mafk, and keep
ftill an ambaffador at our court;
but for my part, I have no doubt of
finifter defigns which will foon appear
evident; and that the ideas of Caftilian honour are phantoms, by which
we muft not fuffer ourfelves to be deceived in a political light, whatever
notions we may have been induced
to form of individuals.

In the courfe of my journey to this
place, I paffed over the plains of
Almanza.

Almanza where a pillar proclaims the victory of the French and Spaniards over the allied army in 1707, when moſt of the Engliſh were killed or taken priſoners, having been ſhamefully abandoned by the Portugueze horſe at the firſt charge, and the ſucceſs of that day fixed the crown of Spain on Philip Duke of Anjou, father to the preſent king, adding new dominions to the reſtleſs and ambitious houſe of Bourbon.

Our ſoldiers ſpilled their blood in that war, as they had done before in that cauſe. In the reign of Charles the II. the Engliſh troops obtained a compleat victory at the battle of Evora, and took the rich tent and all the baggage of Don John of Auſtria,

the

the Spanifh general; for which our Charles generoufly ordered the fum of forty thoufand crowns to be diftributed among the foldiery.—What do you think was the largefs of our magnanimous ally?—Three pounds of fnuff to each company! which when given to the Englifh foldiers, they toffed up in the air out of contempt and difdain (a).

(a) The following paffage from a judicious writer, fhews the obligation of the Portugueze nation to England fo fully, and carries fuch conviction with it, that I am induced to make the quotation. " I have feen, he fays, a large collection of privileges granted by feveral kings of Portugal to the Englifh beyond thofe enjoyed by the Portugueze fubjects, I know not whether I may call them *charters*. Thefe were copied from the archives of the kingdom in the *Torre del Tumbo*, but the moft antient was of king Ferdinand whofe reign began not till 1367. There are feveral of John the Firft, his fucceffor, fome of which

I was

I was mufing on this fubject, and had bewildered myfelf in political reflec-

. refer to others granted by his predeceffors. By this it appears that the Englifh had a great hand in fetting up the kingdom of Portugal, and if the hiftorians of this country deceive us not, they had as great a fhare in protecting and fecuring it, as often as it hath been brought into danger by a foreign enemy. Twice it was like to be wholly over-run by the Caftilians, who had poffeffed themfelves of the greateft part of the kingdom, and gained a numerous party of the nobility over to their fide, and had been very near taking Lifbon itfelf; the firft time in the reign of Ferdinand, the laft of the lawful defcendants from Alfonfo Henriquez, the other time while John the Firft, from whom all that had fucceeded him derived their titles, was ftruggling for the crown, and they have been as often relieved by the Englifh and enabled to carry the war into the enemy's country; our princes of the blood condefcending to go in perfon to their affiftance, firft Edmund Langley Earl of Cambridge, and afterwards John of Gaunt Duke of Lancafter ; and if after the feveral flourifhing reigns that fucceeded, they were at laft reduced under the Spanifh yoke, it was becaufe

tions

tions till I entered the plains of *La Mancha*. There I recovered my good humour; faw many a fat laughing Sancho, drank good wine at *Cuidad Real*, fpent a night at the village *del Toboſo*, the reſidence of the peerleſs Dulcinea; faw the windmills which the diſtracted Quixote miſtook for

they were wanting to themſelves, the Engliſh having ſent out a gallant fleet and army to their refcue, under Don Antonio, whom they had made their king, but they would not accept deliverance, and ſo they remained under the power of their enemies. Thoſe ſmall forces ſent by king Charles, after his reſtoration, by their unparalleled valour, foon put an end to the quarrel, and the victories obtained by their means being feconded, as they were, by the vigilance, dexterity and conduct of the fame king's miniſters, recovered Portugal and reſtored it to the condition in which it now remains." See "An account of the court of Portugal under the reign of the preſent king Don Pedro IId." London, 1700.

giants,

giants, and at a *Venta*, or inn in La Mancha, was pleafed with the fimplicity of a *Manchega* girl, who waited upon me at fupper, and afking her if fhe had ever heard of fuch a perfon as Don Quixote, anfwered, " O yes Sir, often ; they fay he is lately dead." But this will not feem extraordinary when I was told of a field Officer, a perfon of merit, that after long fervice had rifen from a private foldier, who, when in company, and the difcourfe fell on Don Quixote, faid, he had often heard of him, and afked " whether he had not been Colonel of the Regiment of Flanders."

Having been in this capital before, I fpeak with more boldnefs of their manners and cuftoms. You muft not

however

however expect from me details of this fort; or imagine a variety of entertainments, as in London or Paris; or fuch open fcenes of diffipation and luxury as are daily exhibited in thofe brilliant capitals; but though the walk is more private, I believe the inhabitants, whatever they may be in fcience or refinement, are not behind hand with them in vice or debauchery, as they are daily lavifhing the treafures of Mexico and Peru in private amours, and expence, divefted of magnificence or fplendour.

A fet of gay fparks had lately introduced an affembly for dancing, where the manners of the *Adamites* were followed, and blind fidlers were employed for greater precaution.---Thefe

depraved

depraved knights were decorated at thefe revels with a ribband and badge, but they were foon difcovered, and rigoroufly punifhed. If fuch is the depravity of youth, you will naturally fuppofe a liberal and good education is wanting, as well as agreeable and pleafing fociety, added to thofe convivial hours, where the wifeft man need not be afhamed to be feen; but thefe are unknown, and though the Spaniards enjoy fuch a variety of choice, and delicious wines, they feem ignorant of the good qualities of the grape, and if they are feldom taxed with the irregularities of inebriation, they are equally ftrangers to its generous effufions. Their own countryman Roderic Sanchez, bifhop of Palencia, who dedicated his

G   hiftory

hiftory to Henry the 4th, king of Caftile, fays, "that the Spaniards are
more inclined to keep their wine in
the cellar than to drink it, and
chufe rather to fell than partake of
it, and that the fair fex and youth
dread it like poifon(a);" infomuch that
if you except the open hearted Bif-
cayners, and a few boon companions
of honeft Sancho Panza, the circling
glafs is unknown, and the chearful
moment of the poet never thought
of, who faid

"Nunc eft bibendum."----

(a) Vinum quoque malúnt in cellario quam in ven-
tre, quippe qui vendere potius quam guftare præoli-
gunt: fœminæ, vero, & pueri bacchum ut venenum
fugiunt.---Roderici Santii Epifcopi Palentini Hiftoria,
Hifpanica, pars prima, caput iv.

LETTER VII.

Poetry of Galicia and Portugal.

MADRID, 20th JUNE, 1778.

THE plains of Almanza had led me in my laſt letter, into a ſtrain of hiſtorical and military reflections, which imperceptibly drew on a political rant, when I intended to ſpeak to you of the galician and portugueze muſe, previous to my account of the Poets of Caſtile, which you will now expect from me, being at preſent on that claſſic ſpot where the mighty emperor Charles held his court; where many of their beſt poets

G 2   ſung,

fung; where Quevedo befides his diftinguifhed talents as a poet, gave
fuch fhining proofs of refined wit
and profound erudition; and finally,
where the ever admired Cervantes
firft exhibited his unparalleled hero.

The galician mufe was diftinguifhed
at an early period, though her flights
were not lofty, and chiefly fupported
in the caufe of religion, by the numerous votaries who reforted to the
fhrine of St. James, at Compoftella.
The poetical turn prevailed fo far, as
to be the chief employment of both
fexes. King Alfonfo, the wife, received his education in Galicia, and
in that dialect compofed canticles for
the church; which, with other pieces

of the times are preserved in the cathedral of Toledo. Some of them were published by Zuniga the historian, in his annals of Seville, as far as they related to Alfonso's father, Ferdinand the third, who conquered Seville from the Moors. The poems of Macias, a native of Padron in Galicia, were in that dialect, though taken for Portugueze by Argote de Molina. The poet Juan de Mena laments the tragical end of Macias, as does Juan Rodrignez del Padron in his poem of *gozos de Amor,* " Enjoyments of Love," who was so affected at the news of his death that he retired into a convent, where he ended his days. Garci Sanchez de Badojoz, an elegant poet, speaks feelingly of Macias in his poem *Infierno de Amor,* " Hell of Love," and utters a desponding wish to be interred along with him, and share his reputation, which he expresses in the following pathetic stanza,

> Si te plaze, que mis dias
> Yo fenefca mal logrado
> Tan en breve.
>
> Plegate qui con Macias
> Ser merefco fepultado,
> Y decir deve.
>
> Do la fepultara fea,
> Una tierra los crio,
> Una muerte los llevo,
> Una gloria los poffea.

The cataftrophe of this unhappy poet, and the imprudence of his paffion, has afforded a moral tale to all fucceffive bards ; many of his poems

are

are in the *Cancionero de Poetas Anti-
guos* of Juan Alfonſo de Baena, in
the Eſcurial, and give a true idea of
the galician ſtyle of poetry, from
whence we may fairly trace the Portugueze idiom, as the conqueſt and
peopling of Portugal under Henry
of Burgundy, was effected by people
from the north of Galicia, in conjunction with foreigners. Many
places in the north of Portugal acquired the ſame names with thoſe in
Galicia, as it happened in England
after the coming in, of the Saxons ;
Galicia then extended further to the
ſouth, including all thoſe diſtricts
between the rivers Duero, and Min-
ho, which did not appertain to Lu-
ſitania. Ptolemy diſtinguiſhes two
claſſes of people in Galicia, the *Bra-*
G 4

cenſes,

cenſes, whoſe capital was at Braga, and the *Lucenſes* at Lugo. When Portugal was erected into a ſeparate kingdom, they encroached on the borders, ſo that what had belonged to Galicia, now became Portugal, and under their monarchs a new court ſupported a variation, and gave a national character to their language, of which Bluteau, an Engliſhman, and chaplain to Queen Catherine, conſort of our Charles the 2d, has given a moſt ample and learned vocabulary.

The portugueſe muſe made a figure in the 12th century, under Alfonſo, the 1ſt king of Portugal, in whoſe reign Gonzalo Henriquez, and Egas Moniz, are the firſt poets in the records

cords of that kingdom. In the next century, king Dennis was a poet, as was also his natural son Alfonso Sanchez. The 14th century furnished king Alfonso the 4th, a favourite of the muses, whose poems have been collected by father Bernardo Brito. His son king Peter was likewise a poet. In the reign of king John 1st, the Infant Don Pedro composed various sonnets, in praise of Vasco Lobeira, the supposed author of the celebrated romance of *Amadis of Gaul,* of which so much has been said, and who furnished so many admirable scenes to the animated pencil of Cervantes. In the 15th century, Henriquez Cayado distinguished himself under king Emanuel, as did afterwards the Infant Don Pedro, son of king John

2d. At this time the Latin mufe was again invoked by the Portuguefe, and the purity of the Auguftan age feemed to revive with Achilles Stacio, Diego Pereyra, Morais, Coelho, and the jefuit Luis de la Cruz, who wrote fome latin tragedies; which made the hiflorian Faria fay, that in his country every fountain was an Hippocrene, and every hill a Parnaffus. The 16th century produced Bernardino Ribeira, Francifco Saa de Miranda, Michael de Cabedo, the famous comedian Gil Vicente and his daughter Paula, who not only affifled her father in writing his comedies, but alfo compofed others of her own invention. All thefe flourifhed under John IIId. to whom we ought to add the poets under the reign of the unfortunate

king

king Sebaſtian, ſuch as Euſtacio de Faria, Geronimo de Corte Real, Jorge de Montemayor, and above all, the illuſtrious Camoens, whoſe beautiful poem of the Luſiad alone, would have been ſufficient, to perpetuate the poetical character of his country; though Galicia lays a claim to his origin, as deſcended from a family of that kingdom.

The Portugueſe *Cancionero* contains many more poets than the Spaniſh one, as that of Caſtile has only one hundred and twenty poets, and that of Portugal one hundred and fifty; the Spaniſh one, only includes thoſe of the fifteenth century, that of Portugal goes as high as king Peter, who died in 1367. Amongſt others,

of

of this amorous monarch, accept of
the following, addreſſed to the lady
of his affections, whom he ſtiles his
ſecond God.

    Mais dyna de ſer ſervida
    Que ſenhora de eſte mundo !!
    Vos ſoes o meu Debs ſegundo
    Vos ſoes meu bem de eſta vida.

You will think me a book-worm
indeed, for looking ſo far back into
antiquity, and after the indifferent
account I have given you of ſociety in this place, will conclude that
theſe purſuits waſte away all my time,
which might be much better employed ; however I do not neglect
exerciſe, and for this purpoſe have
purchaſed a beautiful Andaluſian

                      gennet

gennet, from a gentleman of Cordova, who boafts of its race. Though he would not win a plate at Newmarket, nor perhaps hold out at a fox chace, with an Englifh hunter; he has neverthelefs numerous qualities that give pleafure to his rider; the docility of his temper, the goodnefs of his mouth, and the agility and quicknefs of his motions, with his elegant fhape, form his principal character, while his flowing mane and well furnifhed tail, added to his ftately carriage, give him a noble and graceful appearance;—his colour *Ifabel*, a name given in allufion to the whimfical vow, and fhift of Ifabella Clara Eugenia, governefs of the Netherlands, at the memorable fiege of Oftend, which lafted from 1601 till 1604,

1604, and who wanted to perſuade
the ladies of her court to follow her
example, which they imitated in
having their linen dyed.---As to the
ſwiftneſs of my courſer I muſt however inform you that he was generated by the wind, and ſo they all
are at Aranjuez, if you will believe
the inſcription over the king's ſtables
at that place *ex vento gravidas*. If
you will not truſt to the king's e-
querry, nor rely upon what has been
ſaid by Varro, or Columella, I muſt
refer you to Virgil,

    - - - - - - - Et ſæpe ſine ullis
Conjugiis vento gravidæ, mirabile dictu
Saxa per, & ſcopulos & depreſſas convalles
Diffugiunt.

GEORG. Lib. 3.

P. S. Excuſe

P. S. Excuse a digreſſion from a Quixotic traveller, in favour of the famous *Roſinante*, though not generated by the wind, and moreover ſo ſteady, that he would not mend his pace if all the mares of the *Deheſa*, or paſtures of Cordova, were in company. In the very firſt chapter, ſpeaking of this ſteed, the text ſays, *Que tenia mas quartos que un Real.* The drift of which conſiſts in a pun, upon the double meaning of the word *Quarto*, which ſignifies a piece of copper money, as well as a defect in a horſe's hoof, and as there are ſeventeen *quartos* in the ſilver coin, called *Real*, it alludes to the numberleſs defects in *Roſinante's* hoof, and cannot be literally tranſlated. This paſſage greatly puzzled Peter Motteux, the

publiſher

publisher of a translation of Don Quixote, by several hands, in 1733, who
alters the sense of it by rendering
it thus, " Whose bones stuck out
" like the corners of a Spanish real."
I suppose he had seen some of the
old cut Spanish money which sug-
gested this erroneous idea. Smollet
has continued the same blunder, and
learnedly added by way of note, that
a Spanish real is a coin of a very ir-
regular shape not unlike the figure
in geometry, called *Trapezium*.

I have now on my table a treatise
on farriery, by one of the king's far-
riers, *The Gibson* of Spain, entitled,
*Instituciones de albeyteria por el Bachiller
Francisco Garcia Cabrera, herrador, y al-
beytar de las cavallerizas del Rey.* Madrid

drid 1775. In which he gives the following account of the *quarto*. " To explain the reafon why this accident is called by the name of a *quarto* I am perplexed, not being certain, nor convinced by the reafons given me by different perfons; fome fay it is becaufe it falls upon the fourth part of the hoof, others, becaufe the animal by this means lofes the fourth part of its value; to the firft I anfwer, that I am unacquainted with the exact dimenfions of a *quarto*; to the fecond that if the accident is of the compound kind, though the animal was ever fo valuable before, it becomes then not only not worth a *quarto*, but not even an *ochavo*."

LETTER VIII.

Origin and progress of national poetry in Castile.

TOLEDO, 29th June, 1778.

I HAVE made an excursion to the city of Toledo, twelve leagues south of Madrid, and dignified with the title of imperial, after its conquest from the Moors, by Alfonso the 6th, who stiled himself emperor, and was crowned here; since which the city has bore for their armorial ensigns, an emperor seated in a royal chair in his robes, holding a drawn sword in his right hand, and a mund in his left.

I shall

I fhall leave to travel writers to defcribe the numerous edifices and public ftructures, as well as churches, pictures, and ftately monuments to be feen in this place. The cathedral alone would require a volume; amongft its many fuperb tombs, I particularly noticed that of Don Alvaro de Luna, conftable of Caftile, the unfortunate favourite of king John 2d, and that of Cardinal Mendoza, archbifhop of Toledo, fon to that illuftrious poet, the Marquifs of Santillana. With refpect to the variety of ornaments in this antient cathedral, the critic has a noble field of matter; as for the unwieldy groupe of figures in this church, fo much admired by the inhabitants, and called, I know not for what rea-

 fon,

ſon, *El Tranſparente*; one of their own writers, Don Antonio Ponz, a modern critic, fairly acknowledges, " That for any uſe or ornament, it affords, this immenſe maſs of marble might as well have remained buried for ever in the quarry of Carrara !" I ſhall ſay nothing of the badneſs and crooked form of the ſtreets, ſtill more inconvenient from the ſituation of the city on a hill, much leſs can be offered in favour of the environs of Toledo, which are bleak and in great want of trees, though Martial, in one of his epigrams to Licinius, repreſents the country in his time, on the bank of the Tagus, to have been much favoured with ſhade.

> Æſtus ſerenos aureo franges Tago
> Obſcurus umbris arborum.

But

. But it is now high time to proceed on my favourite ſubject.—When the Latin tongue, which had been univerſal in Spain, became totally corrupted by ſuch different invaſions, and variety of nations, and diſpoſitions, the Caſtilian language is ſuppoſed to have infenſibly aroſe about the 12th century.—The oriental poetry had flouriſhed near five hundred years, and the Provenzal and Galician dialects about one hundred, ſo that when the genius of Caſtilian poetry firſt began to expand and acquire a national form, it muſt have borrowed of courſe from the ſpirit of its predeceſſors, and had its origin, like all antient languages, in ſinging the exploits of heroes, ſounding forth the praiſe of the Deity, and tuning

H 3

their

their lyre to the cause of religion: such were their *Cantares*, of which the *Cancioneros* have preserved ample collections.—I have enlarged upon the style and character of these several people, in order to form from thence some fixed idea, or rule proper to be assigned, as an origin to the poetry of Castile, tracing the sources of its singular variety, and discovering that want of unity in its character, in proportion as it has imitated such a diversity of models. The oriental style in the first place, delights in strained allusions, and extravagant metaphors, adorned with exuberance of expression, and an admirable variety and brilliancy of sentiment: it is happy in the harmony of its numbers, and when it rises to solemn and majestic

subjects

fubjects, is faid to lofe itfelf in enthufiafm and rapture. The Provenzal
poetry on the other hand is reftricted
by the laws of the Trobadours, and
being fettered in the golden chains
of love, becomes languid and faint,
when it attempts to defcribe the
thunder of Jove, or the anger of military heroes, with the clangour of
war.

Such was the flock from whence
the Caftilian bee was to draw an
inexhauftible ftore, and to fip every
flower, inriching itfelf with a fund
that was to charm future ages, and
convey to the mind the moft perma-
nent and pleafing fenfations. When
they followed the manner of the ori-

H 4

ental

entals, the Trobadours, or the Italians, it proceeded from a natural im-
pulfe, which leads to imitate the objects conftantly in view; when they
copied the Greeks, and Romans, it
owed its effect to a more refined and
elevated genius.----The various objects of the bards fucceffively altered
with the times; the atchievements
of Charlemagne and the twelve peers
of France, drew the attention of the
French and Italians; then came the
croifades and the feats of knights
infpired with a military zeal for religion; after thefe were at an end, the
mind was ftill exalted and attached
to the marvellous, fuited to the pre-
vailing manners, fo that the fictitious
heroes and knight errants eafily fucceeded, and the tale was embellifhed

with

with the amorous novel, in which the Spanish warriors were introduced with such a delusive medley of falsehood and truth, that some have taken fable for history, and others have rejected fact for romance. At last a surprising genius arose, the universal admiration of mankind, who with the invincible lance of Don Quixote, drove for ever all those extravagant heroes out of the field.

As music is composed of certain tones and cadences, it was necessary that what was to be sung should have a proper metre adapted to musical harmony, from whence the first origin of verse, in every part of the world; that the Spanish language is admirably adapted to poetic harmony,

ny, has been generally allowed, and
has been evidently proved by an excellent judge, Francifco Salinas, of
Burgos, born in 1513, celebrated by
his contemporaries for his great fkill in
mufic, as a performer and a theorift ;
and though afflicted with blindnefs
from his infancy, inftead of depreff-
ing his mind, it tended to improve
his mufical genius in a wonderful
manner.   He went to Rome in the
retinue of Don Pedro Sarmiento,
archbifhop of Compoftella, and after
twenty years fpent in Italy, returned
to Salamanca, where he held a pro-
fefforfhip of mufic, and died at the
age of feventy-feven, univerfally admired and regretted.

In tracing then the poetry of Caftile through its various modulations
from

from its origin down to the prefent time, we may divide it into four periods; the firft from its early dawn till the reign of king John the 2d; the next from this king to the days of Charles the 5th; the third from that emperor down to Philip the 4th; and the laft from that reign down to Charles the 2d, the laft Auftrian monarch, when the genius of Homer and Virgil feems to have fled from the banks of the Manzanares, and to have fixed its refidence on thofe of the Thames. In this manner its firft ftate may be compared to its infancy, the fecond to its juvenile days, the third to its vigour and manhood, and the fourth to its old age and de-cline.

The

The Caſtilian bard made his firſt effort in an age when there was little refinement in language, and the ear unaccuſtomed to melodious ſounds, or ſkilful enough to be affeſted by the harmonious numbers of the antients, much leſs in a ſituation to imitate them. The moſt antient poet known in Caſtile is not of a higher date than the beginning of the thirteenth century. This is Gonſalo Berceo, native of the town of Berceo, in Guypuſcoa and a monk of the convent of St. Milan, from whoſe archives it appears that he lived in 1220, he wrote the lives of St. Milan, St. Dominic of Silos, and other Spaniſh ſaints in verſe, of twelve, thirteen and fourteen ſyllables, as well as a poem on the battle of Simancas,

where

where the Moors were defeated by
Ramiro the 2d, king of Leon. Thefe
with fome others are in manufcript,
in the convent of St. Milan. There
is likewife a poem of his on the mafs
in the royal library at Madrid, but
nothing more has been printed than
his life of St. Dominic, wherein he ac-
quaints his readers that he attempted his poem in Spanifh, being totally unable to perform it in Latin.

> Quiero fer una profa en roman paladino
> En qual fuele el pueblo fablar a vecino
> Ca non fo tan letrado por fer otro latino.

The fimilitude and analogy obferved between the latin and Spanifh verfe, fuch as the verfe of eight
feet with the Trocaic, that of five
with the Adonic, that of eleven with

the

the Sapphic Asclepediad, or Choriambic, and other similar compositions, shew their origin from the greek and latin models; but with respect to imitation, we must rather look for it amongst the Trobadours and Italians, from whom they borrowed the *Soneto, Madrigal, Cancion, Terceto, Octava Rima*, and similar poems, different from the ancient *Coplas* of Spain.

The *Coplas*, called *Redondillas*, or Roundelays, are of great antiquity. The Spanish poets of those days, when they wrote in latin, made use of the rhyme of the roundelays, and from them perhaps it was adopted in the national poetry. An epitaph in the

the church of Toledo, of the year 1333, has the following lines.

Mitibus hic mitis, tamen hoftibus effe ftudebat
Hoftis, fulgebat propter certamina litis.

Which divided by the *Cefura* of rhyme, would run thus.

Mitibus hic mitis,
Tamen hoftibus effe ftudebat
Hoftis, fulgebat
Propter certamina litis.

Another epitaph in the fame church :

Toleti natus, cujus generofa propago
Moribus ornatus fuit hic probitatis imago:
Largus, magnificus, electus mendomenfis,
Donis inmenfis, cunctorum verus amicus.

Which divided in the fame manner, will be,

Toleti

Toleti natus,
Cujus generofa propago
Moribus ornatus
Fuit hic probitatis imago
Largus, magnificus
Electus Mendionenfis,
Donis inmenfis
Cunctorum verus amicus.

In the early days of their poetry, we often find verfe of four, five, fix and eight fyllables, in the works of the infant Don Manuel, who died in 1362, and alfo made ufe of the Hendecafyllable verfe, as did the marquis of Santillana.

The verfes of twelve fyllables were ftyled *De arte major*, and were ufed by king Alfonfo the Wife, in his poem of *Las querelas*, or " Complaints" againft the rebellion of his undutiful fon Sancho ; but the verfe of thirteen

teen and fourteen feet are the moſt ancient metre, being uſed by Berceo the monk, and king Alfonſo above-mentioned.

As to rhyme, we know it exiſted before the Goths extended them-ſelves to the ſouth, or the Saracens penetrated into the weſt: it has been thought by ſome writers, that even in the Auguſtan age the poets had a partiality for rhyme at the end, like the Leonine verſe, inſtances of which are ſeen in Horace (a), O-vid (b), Propertius (c), and Marti-

(a) Non ſatis eſt pulchra eſſe poemata dulcia ſunto
Et quocumque volent, animum auditoris agunto.
ART. POET.

(b) Quot cœlum ſtellas, tot habet tua Roma puellas.
DE ART AMAND. LIB. I.

(c) Nec tibi tirrhena ſolvatur funis arena.
LIB. I. ELEG. 17.

I   al (a),

al (a), and the similsonance was con-
sidered as a figure of rhetoric.---How-
ever that might have been, the
monkish writers, without any feeling
for the true graces of poetry, were
delighted with jingling sounds, thinking with confonance and rhyme to
supply the place of genius and fancy.
To perceive the similitude between
their barbarous latin verfe and the
Spanish rhyme of thofe days, we have
only to compare them together.---An
epitaph in the cathedral of Toledo,
of 1326, is as follows :

Hoc pofitus tumulo fuit expers improbitatis,
Intus & extra fuit immenfœ probitatis,
Largus, magnificus fuit, & dans omnia gratis,
Et fpeculum generis, totius fons bonitatis.

(d) Diligo præflantem, non odi cinna negantem.

Lib. 7. Epig. 42.

This

This ſtrophe preſerves the ſame rhyme, as thoſe of the monk Berceo, with reſpect to the conſonance of the four verſes.---Let us now compare ·it with a Spaniſh epitaph of the year 1388.

D. Sancho óbiſpo de avila como ſenor honrado,
Dio muy buen exemplo, como fue buen prelado,
Fizo eſte monaſterio de S. Benito llamado
Y diole muy grandes algos, por do es ſubſtentado.

Verſes ending with an echo were uſed by Juan de la Encina, and are with his other poems in the *Cancionero general* printed at Seville, in 1535. The laſt part of the penultimate word is echoed by a ſimilar one, thus,

El mas querido, y inflamado, amado,
Pueſto en el duro, y ſin conſuelo, ſuelo,
Sufre por mi, de tierra y cielo, yelo,
En un peſebre defechado, echado.

many

Many new kind of verſe, ſuch as ſapphic, adonic, phaleucian and o-thers, were introduced by Bermudez, in his tragedies of *Nize*. The verſe called *Eſdrujulo* was firſt uſed by Cayraſco de Figueroa, and always ends with dactyls, or words that have the accent on the antipenultimate ſyllable, with the two laſt ſyllables ſhort, thus,

Al prado de ſan Geronimo
Con mis zelos, y mi cantaro.
Salgo a vengarme de un picaro
Que nove el eſtilo xacaro.

Vicente Eſpinel is commonly ſaid to be the inventor of the verſes called after him *Eſpinelas,* but this is contro-verted by Don Gregorio Mayans, who attributes them to Juan Angel, who uſed them in his poem of *Tragitriumſo*

in

in 1523, and only allows to Efpinel the merit of having improved the metre. Efpinel alfo wrote a romance under the feigned name of *El Efcudero Marcos de Obregon*, defcribing the fol-lies of his youth, from whence the French writer La Sage has interwoven feveral of his characters in his romance of Gil Blas.

Other verfes were called *Felicianas*, according to Lopez de Vega, from the inventrefs of that name, who fpent fome time in men's apparel in the univerfity of Salamanca.---It would be an ufelefs tafk to relate the variety of inven-tions which fprang up in a barbarous age, fuch as the retrogade verfe, the labyrinth, the cento, the acroftic, and other puerile fancies, of which Cara-

muel,

mucl, a Spanish monk in the laſt cen-tury, has compiled two folio volumes under the title of *Rythmica* and *Metramica*, which were reprinted in Italy: but I will not take up more of your time with ſuch trifles, and haſten to ſpeak of blank verſe, which is of great antiquity in Spain, where they ſeem as ſenſible of its dignity and majeſty as we are in England. They had it at the ſame time that the famous Triſſino firſt introduced it in Italy, for his contemporary Alónſo de Fuentes, of Seville, publiſhed a poem there in 1547, in blank verſe, intitled *La Suma de Philoſophia*. Triſſino died in 1550.

I this moment receive the agreeable news of your ſafe return to England.

land. The melancholy account you
give me of parties, and faction at
home, grieves me exceedingly; but
I truſt in the ſpirit of our people and
our numerous reſources to overcome
both foreign and domeſtic enemies.
Foreign nations, unacquainted with
our conſtitution and government, and
who only hear the miſrepreſentations
and clamour of faction, imagine we
are undone; the French flatter themſelves to have in a manner ſecured to
themſelves, the poſſeſſion of America, under the veil of an alliance with
the congreſs; and the Spaniards fondly conceive that Gibraltar will fall an
eaſy prey into their hands; how egre-
giouſly they are deceived in this, as well
as in their romantic ideas of conquer-

ing

ing Jamaica, I truſt to providence and our own vigorous exertions to ſhew! you tell me we have a fine fleet in the Bay. under the command of an experienced officer, who, if he falls in with the enemy, no doubt will give a good account of them, and, I hope, return home, crowned with laurels, to receive the thanks of his countrymen. Methinks I ſee the gallant veteran entering London in triumph, like a Roman conſul, with the ſpoils of the enemy, amidſt the ſhouts and acclamations of a grateful people, repeating inceſſantly his victories! I muſt ſay no more, poets you know, are apt to have viſions, let me wiſh this may be a true one, and that in all parts of the world our

fleets

fleets and arms may ever be victorious, and, to ufe the expreffion of a great writer, "affert triumphantly the rights and honour of Great-Britain, as far as waters roll, and as winds can waft them."

Adieu !

LETTER IX.

King Alfonso the Wise improves the Spanish Language.----Singular poem of the archpriest of Hita.

TOLEDO, 12th July, 1778.

I AM defirous, whilft in this city, of faying fomething more to you of the royal poet Alfonfo, the 10th king of Caftile, who held his court here, and was firnamed the Wife, on account of his great learning and knowledge of aftronomy. It was here that he caufed thofe famous aftronomical tables to be drawn up, called Alfonfine, after his name, which are

carefully

carefully preferved in the cathedral
of Seville.---He perfected the Spanish
code, named *Las Siete Partidas*, from
their being divided into feven parts,
correfponding with the feven letters
of his name. He moreover introduced the national language into all
public[10] writings ; an example which
was foon after followed with us, by
our Edward the 3d, who gave orders for the abolifhing of the Norman
tongue in all public acts and judi-
cial proceedings.

King Alfonfo caufed a great many
books to be tranflated into the Caftilian language, and befides giving
the example by feveral compofitions
of his own in profe and verfe, he,
fpent large fums of money for the

advancement

advancement of science, and extended his bounty and generosity on all occasions with the utmost magnificence.---Amongst other extraordinary performances of this great king, there is a poem written in 1272, called *Thesoro*, which is in the royal library of Madrid, being a treatise on the philosopher's stone, written in cyphers, and in magical characters. This book is thought to have belonged to the library of the marquis of Villena, and to have been one of those saved by the bishop of Segovia. Gil Gonzales de Avila, in his history of the church of Seville, has given the introduction to this work in Spanish verse, in which the royal poet says he had invited a famous chemist from Alexandria, in Egypt, to teach

him

him the art of making gold, which
they had frequently practiſed together, and had acquired a perfect
knowledge of the philoſopher's ſtone.
The verſe runs thus.

La piedra que llaman philoſophal
Sabia facer, e me la enſeno.
Fizimos la juntos; deſpues ſolo yo,
Conque muchas veres crecio mi caudal,
E viendo que puede facerſe eſta tal,
De muchas maneras, mas ſiempre una coſa
Yo vos propongo la menos penoſa,
Por mas excelente, e mas principal (a).

Amongſt other numerous works of
this ſovereign, there is a folio manu-

(a) That is—he knew how to make the philoſopher's ſtone, and taught it me. We made it together, and I afterwards made it by myſelf, ſo that I
often increaſed my ſtock; and finding that it is to
be made in different ways, but always one and the
ſame thing, I propoſe to you the leaſt expenſive, as
the compleateſt and beſt method.

ſcript,

script, in the library of Toledo, written on paper in Spanish, on miscellaneous subjects. Amongst the rest, a tract relating to St. Patrick's Purgatory, in Ireland, which perhaps may be the origin of the famous vision of Odænius, mentioned by some Irish writers. Alfonso is thought to have first introduced paper in Spain, at least amongst the Christians, supposing its use to have been known amongst the Mahometans; for Sarmiento mentions having seen a paper manuscript in 1261. I shall not, however, enter into further details relating to the works of this monarch, he was a competitor for the empire, with Richard Duke of Cornwall, who was chosen emperor, but not having fortune or

power

power fufficient to fupport its dignity, was obliged to return to England,
and they elected another prince. As
for king Alfonfo, his expences reduced him to great ftraights; nor
could his fuppofed knowledge of the
philofopher's ftone, furnifh gold e-
nough without laying heavy taxes on
his fubjects : while this monarch was
bent upon aftronomical purfuits, inftead of the intereft of his people,
and in lieu of obferving the motions
of his fubjects, was watching thofe
of the ftars in the crown of Ariadne;
his fecond fon Sancho rebelled againft
him, fnatched his own crown from
his head, and got poffeffion of the
kingdom. For this undutiful act, and
his fucceffive victories over the Moors,

the

the Spanish historians have called him
Don Sancho El Bravo (a).

(*a*) Alfonso the Wise had two sons. Ferdinand the
eldest and Sancho. The former died in the life time
of his father, and the latter usurped the crown, on
which his nephew Alfonso, Ferdinand's son, then
a minor, fled to France, and was proclaimed king on
the death of Alfonso the Wise, but Sancho's party
prevailed. This Alfonso firnamed *La Cerda*, from a
long hair on his back, married Maude of France, and
left a fon, Lewis, who returned to Spain, and ceding
his right to the crown, accepted lands from king Ferdinand the 4th, and married Leonora Guzman,
daughter of Alonfo Perez de Guzman, founder of
the ducal-houfe of Medina Sidonia, by whom he
left an only daughter, *Ifabella La Cerda*, firft married
to Don Rodrigo Alvarez de Afturias, by whom fhe
had no iffue, and afterwards to Bernard de Bearne,
baftard fon of the famous Gafton Phæbus Count
de Foix Lord of Bearne ; on this marriage de Bearne
was created Count of Medina Celi, and a large eftate
fettled on Ifabella his wife, in 1367, by Henry the
2d, firnamed the Baftard, on condition of her re-
nouncing again for herfelf and her heirs, all preten-

A fingular

A fingular poet and fatyrift now occurs, who has efcaped the refearches of Don Nicolas Antonio, and moft other biographers, till difcovered by Don Lewis Velazquez, knight of the order of St. James. This is Juan Ruiz, arch-prieft of Hita, whofe works are in manufcript, in the library of Toledo, and who flourifhed in the year 1330. The manufcript is in a very imperfect condition, with many fheets tore out, and others unintelligible, therefore I fhall confine myfelf to a fpecimen of a fatyrical piece, as given by Velafquez.

fions to the crown of Caftile, as grand daughter of Alfonfo, proclaimed king at the death of Alfonfo the Wife. Afterwards Don Lewis de Bearne the 5th, Count of Medina Celi, defcended from Ifabella, was created Duke of Medina Celi in 1491, by Ferdinand and Ifabel.

K

This

This poem defcribes a conteft between the time of *Ealing Meat* and *Lent Time*, wherein the former is defeated on *Aſh Wedneſday*, and remains in a dejected ftate till Holy-week, when recovering his fpirits, he enters the lifts and fends a challenge to *Lent*, by his fecond *Don Breakfaſt*, fixing the time for combat on Eafter-Sunday. *Lent*, not thinking himfelf obliged to receive a challenge from one whom he has vanquifhed, finding himfelf moreover enfeebled, and not being able to procure a frefh fupply of fea fifh, to recruit his conftitution, promifes to meet him at Jerufalem, dreffes himfelf like a pilgrim and makes his efcape on Holy-Saturday. Two potent emperors arrive in the world; *Don Fleſh* and *Dcn Love*. They both

make

make a triumphal entry: the various mufical inftruments are defcribed, as well as the reception they meet with, from all ranks of people; a conteft arifes concerning who is to receive *Don Love*: each party offers his rea-fons and claim for a preference, but he refufes them, and fhews a predi-lection to the author, as an old fer-vant of the family, and goes to his houfe; but the apartments being too fmall for fuch fplendid guefts, a tent is fixed, and here a poetical defcrip-tion is given of the four feafons of the year, in the nature of a vifion. The author, with the confidence of an old fervant, enquires of *Don Love*, where he had been during his ab-fence? he anfwers, in the mild cli-mate of Andalufia during winter, and

 complains

complains, that coming to Toledo in the beginning of lent, they had fhut the gates of the city againft him; on which he applied to feveral convents, but none would receive him, and at laft was obliged to pafs the lent in the town of Caftro, where he was kind-ly entertained. Finally recovering his ftrength after lent, he went to the fair of Alcala, and from thence wan-dering about the country, had left the author in a melancholy mood, who not pleafed with a folitary life, confulted an old trot, called *Trota Conventos*. This forry old woman ad-vifes him to make love to a nun, and paints the delight of fuch amours. *Trota Conventos* applies to a nun, to whom fhe had rendered former fervices, fpeaks in favour of the

archprieft,

archprieft, and acts as procurefs between them. A long dialogue en-
fues, with the perfuafions of the old
Jezabel on one fide, and the refiftance
and inconveniences alledged by the
nun on the other. *Trota Conventos*
difplays the character of the arch-
prieft ;—the nun at laft confents to
receive him on honourable terms,
and dies in two months. The arch-
prieft is much grieved, and engages
the old hag to procure him a wife,
fhe finds out a moor, who refufes the
offer---the author relates the fongs he
had compofed for jews and moors,
adapted to various inftruments, and
proper for dances, and to be fung by
blind men and ftrollers.—*Trota Conventos* dies, the ravages of death are
defcribed, as well as the ingratitude

of relations and heirs. The epitaph
of *Trota Conventos* is given. Preven-
tatives are offered againſt the ſudden
acts of death, which are to be guarded againſt with the ſhield of good
works.

' Such is the main ſcope of this
whimſical poem, many parts of which
are unintelligible at preſent. One
of the laſt verſes ſays expreſſly that it
was finiſhed in the year 1378.—The
work is not deſtitute of poetical invention, and ſeems to be a violent
ſatyr on the times, abounding with
moral reflections, as well as lively de-
ſcriptions of the vices of ſome of the
principal perſonages of the court.
At the ſame time the poet ſeems to
laugh in his eaſy chair, and might have

furniſhed

furnifhed a model for Rabelais, who probably never faw this ‚poem:— from the freedom with which the archprieft has painted the vices of the times, we may call him the Petronius of Spain. Some of his verfes have the fame metre as the greek and latin hexameters, for inftance,

Fis vos pequeno libro, de téfta mas que de glofa,
Non creo que es pequeno, ant es mui gran plofa.

The prefent archbifhop of Toledo, Don Francifco de Laranzana has very generoufly opened the library of the cathedral for the ufe of the public, and I might mention other ancient poets, whofe works are in the *Cancionero* of Juan Alfonfo de Baena, collected in the reign of king John the 2d, which includes thofe who pre-

K 4   ceded

ceded, as well as contemporary poets;
but it would make no amends for the
time loft in looking over fuch writings, totally divefled of genius or
tafte, hardly one of them able even
to make a good rhyme; you will already have perceived that I partake
of the gloom that hangs over this
city; or, as the French call it, *ennui*.
Its very gates feem to proclaim it, for
over the principal one, the gate *del
Cambron*, an infcription is placed under the flatue of St. Leocadia, the
tutelary patronefs of the city, in which
fhe is requefted to free them from fuch
a complaint :

> Tu noftra civis inclita,
> Tu es patrona vernula,
> Ab urbis hujus termino
> Procul repelle tædium.

LETTER

LETTER X.

Second period of Spanish Poetry in the 15th century.---Character of King John the second, and of his son King Henry the fourth of Castile.

MADRID, 20th JULY, 1778.

AS the heats begin to be exceffive here, I fhall foon make an excurfion to St. Ildefonfo, a royal feat which ftands in a very high fituation amidft the Guadarrama mountains, that are covered with fnow till the middle of June: there the court enjóy a cool and pleafant fummer, and behold a fecond fpring after their departure from Aranjuez, which they generally leave towards the end of

June

June. In autumn they remove again to the Efcurial, fpend part of the winter in the new palace at Madrid, and are occafionally at the *Cafa del Campo*, a fmall villa near Madrid; or at the *Pardo*, about two leagues from hence; and thus with the different hunting parties of the feafon; thefe regal conftellations perform their annual orbits with great punctuality and famenefs.---On fuch occafions, every thing is extravagantly dear at thefe places; which becomes a heavy charge upon all the foreign minifters, whofe duty obliges them to attend on the monarch; and fince Lord Rochford's time I underftand an extraordinary allowance is made to our ambaffadors for this purpofe.---Let me now make a retrogade move-

ment,

ment, and recall your attention to the court of John the second, king of Caſtile, ſon of Henry the third and Catharine daughter of John of Gaunt, duke of Lancaſter, by Conſtance of Caſtile. Under this prince we may properly fix the ſecond period of Spaniſh poetry, in the fifteenth century, and I ſhall juſt give you a ſlight ſketch of ſome of the principal characters of his court. The king himſelf was a great favourite of the muſes and an excellent judge of poetical merit; he underſtood and ſpoke latin fluently, and was not only a good poet, but moreover, encouraged all thoſe that excelled in that art, delighting in the converſation of men of genius and talents; under ſuch a Mecenas, no wonder that the nobles

ſhould

should follow the royal example, and the palace of king John refemble the court of Apollo: but with all thefe amiable qualities, this indolent prince fuffered himfelf to be governed by his favourites and minions, which brought on him the hatred of his fubjects, who fhewed their fpirit of refentment to fuch a degree, that the king caufed his Privado, Don Alvaro de Luna, to be beheaded at Vallado-lid.----I fhall fay nothing more of the marquis of Villena, as he lived in retirement under this reign, where we find Fernan Perez de Guzman, Lord of Barres, who was both an hiftorian and a poet; the printed *Cancioneros* abound with his works, and fome are in the manufcript one of Juan Alfonfo de Baena; he is author of a poem in-

titled

titled *Las sentencias y coplas de bien vivir*, printed at Lisbon in 1564, and also published the chronicle of king John. He likewise wrote in prose the lives of all the great men who flourished in that king's reign in arms, or letters, intitled *Claros varones Espanoles*, a book greatly esteemed : In its imitation Fernando del Pulgar afterwards writ another, dedicated to Isabella queen of Castile, printed at Madrid in 1678, at the end of the epitome of the chronicle of king John the second. —— Guzman had for contemporary that illustrious nobleman Don Inigo Lopez de Mendoza, marquis of Santillana, who lived till the time of Henry the fourth, son to John the second. By order of king John he drew up a collection of moral

ral proverbs for the inſtruction of prince Henry his ſon, and for the ſame purpoſe alſo wrote a treatiſe on favourites, intitled *Doctrinal de privados*, in which Don Alvaro de Luna is repreſented as ſpeaker, and gives advice to his ſucceſſor, how he ſhould behave like a good miniſter, and not follow his treacherous example.---He likewiſe made a collection of antient proverbs in the Spaniſh language, which were reprinted with other curious pieces of Spaniſh literature in 1737, by Don Gregorio Mayans.---- The marquis ſupported a literary correſpondence with the lord high conſtable of Portugal, Don Pedro, ſon of the Infant Don Pedro, duke of Coimbra ; at the requeſt of this prince, he wrote him a long letter,

ſending

sending him a collection of his poems, and giving him a circumstantial account of the state of poetry in Spain. Father Labbe says, that amongst the king of France's manuscripts, they possess several of the marquis's poems and letters. All the great men of his time were desirous of a literary correspondence with him. Don Gomez Manrique, a great poet, and brother to Don Roderic, first Count of Paredes, and uncle to Don George Manrique, another celebrated poet, wrote a poem to the marquis, requesting his works, and composed several others in his praise. This great man died in 1458, to the great regret of all his acquaintance. The famous poet Juan de Mena particularly laments this event in a poem

he

em he wrote on the occafion, intitled *Coronacion*, wherein he fuppofed himfelf to have been carried up to Parnaffus, and feen the mufes and virtues crown the marquis with laurels, and with much elegance fings his praifes as a philofopher, a poet, a foldier, and a chriftian.

The firft Duke of Infantado was fon to this illuftrious Marquis, and directed in his will, that all the poems of his father, as well as his library, fhould be intailed in the family along with the eftate, and be preferved in his palace of Guadalaxara, where it is faid there is a very curious collection of manufcripts. This ducal family has built at Guadalaxara a fumptuous chapel to depofit the re-

mains

mains of their anceſtors, in imitation of that famous one at the Eſcurial; and is alſo called a pantheon; it contains twenty-ſix urns arranged in proper order, with a great profuſion of curious marble, and coſt 1,082,770 reals vellon, or £12181.

After having ſaid ſo much of the marquis of Santillana, I come to the great Juan de Mena, of Cordova, his friend, whoſe poetical talents were ſo admired by king John, that he retained him conſtantly at his court, and would frequently correct his verſes with his own hand. The moſt celebrated piece of this poet is his *Labyrintho*, in three hundred *octavas*, from whence it is called *Las tres cientas de Juan de Mena*, divided into ſeven

L

parts

parts according to the planets, beginning with the moon, and finishing
with saturn, which has been learnedly commented upon by Fernan
Nunez de Guzman, stiled *El Pinciano,*
to distinguish him from the historio-
grapher I before mentioned. Mena's
poems have gone through a variety
of editions, the oldest was printed at
Sarragossa in 1515. That of Seville
in 1528 contains more poems, and
they were reprinted at Antwerp in
1552.

I must mention a very polite and
accomplished gentleman, who just
reached the days of King John ; his
prose compositions are estimable for
their antiquity, as well as purity and
elegance of language. This was Pedro

dro Lopez de Ayala. He translated Livy into Spanish, much about the time that it first appeared in French by Peter Berchorius, a Benedictine monk. He also translated, from the Italian. the fall of princes of Boccacio, and the Trojan history of Guido Colonna ; Boetius *de Confolatione Philofophiæ*, and Ifidore *de Summo Bono*. He lived under four kings, Peter, Henry 2d, John 1ft, and Henry 3d, of all which he compiled the chronicles; the three firft were printed, but that of Henry the 3d is ftill in manuscript, in the convent of St. Martin, in Madrid. In this work there is an original letter, from Bajazet to Henry 3d, which occafioned the famous embaffy to Tamerlane, by Henry, who fent Ruy Gonzales de Clavijo, as his

L 2

ambaffador

ambaſſador to that ſovereign, an account of which was publiſhed by
Argote de Molina.---Ayala is taxed
with great partiality and flattery in
favour of the rebel Henry againſt his
brother king Peter, whom he ſtabbed
with his own hand, and then uſurp-
ed his dominions. The true chronicle of Peter was written by John de
Caſtro biſhop of Jaen, but was ſup-
preſſed by the partizans of Henry,
after he came to the throne.-----Be-
fore I take my leave of king John, let
me mention another writer that will
afford you much entertainment,
that is the bachelor Fernan Gomez
de Ciudad Real, who was forty-four
years phyſician to king John 2d, and
of courſe well acquainted with all the
intrigues of his court; his letters
were

were publifhed at Burgos in 1499, and throw great light on many actions of the principal characters of his time. This book was lately reprinted at Madrid (*a*). There is a letter amongft them from the poet Juan de Mena, complaining of the behaviour of the bifhop of Cuenca, in burning and fecreting the books of the marquifs of Villena (*b*).

(*a*) Centon epiftolario de Gomez de Ciudad Real, generaciones y Semblanzas de Perez de Gufman : claros varones de Caftilla y letras de F. del Pulgar. Madrid 1775.

(*b*) In a former letter I faid it was the bifhop of Segovia, who burned the books of the marquifs of Villena, mifled by a modern Spanifh writer, when I fhould have faid, that it was Don Lope Barrientos bifhop of Cuenca. Juan de Mena tells us he burned a hundred books by order of the king, and fecreted many others.—He defires Gomez to fend him a letter to be fhewn to the king, in order to get the books

The

The depravity of the age gave rise to another satyrist, whose verse is mentioned in Don Quixote, under the feigned name of *Coplas de Mingo Revulgo*, a satyrical poem, written in a pastoral dialogue, consisting of thirty-five stanzas between the shepherd *Mingo*, or *Dominic*, and *Gil Arebato*, describing the vices of king Henry the fourth, son to John the second, reproaching him as a bad shepherd, who took no care of his flock. The fluttering shepherd, *Tartamudo*, is Moses, *Christoval Mexia* is the Messiah, and the *Meco Moro* is Mahomet. All

again out of the bishop's hands, who he adds had seen no more of the books than the king of Morocco. Mena is very solicitous for the character of the marquifs, that the remains of his library should not fall to so unworthy an heir, who had so little respect for his fame.

their

their flocks are reprefented as graz-
ing promifcuoufly, without any regulation or government, to the ruin and
downfall of the kingdom, in which
Chriftians, Jews, and Mahometans,
lived intermixed, without controul
or fubordination ; for thus we muft
underftand the tenth couplet.

Moderrado con el fueno
No lo cura de almagrar,
Porque no entiende de dar
Cuenta de ello a ningun dueno.
Quanto yo no amoldaria
Lo de Chriftoval Mexia,
Ni del otro tartamudo,
Ni del Meco Moro agudo:
Todo va por una via!

Some have attributed this poem to
Juan de Mena, others to Fernan del
Pulgar, of which opinion is the hifto-

rian

rian Mariana; and when we confider the comment of Pulgar, always printed along with the poem, explaining the moſt obſcure paſſages, it ſeems to be a probable conjecture. As to the vices of Henry the fourth, they exceed the pen of the moſt poignant ſatyriſt. He ſtands charged with having conſented to the infidelity of his queen, with Betran de la Cueva, who for recompence was created count of Ledeſma. The princeſs Jane was ſuppoſed to be the iſſue of this amour; her legitimacy was publicly conteſted, which occaſioned much bloodſhed, and ended in her being obliged to retire to a convent, ſtigmatized with the name of *La Bertrandina*; and Henry's ſiſter Iſabella became heireſs of the crown of Caſtile,

tile, which by her marriage with Ferdinand of Aragon, became united for ever to that kingdom.

We now draw near to a more polished age, and to new events under the aufpicious reign of Ferdinand and Ifabel; another great genius appears on the horizon, the poet Juan de la Encina, who went to Jerufalem with the marquis of Tarifa, and has defcribed that expedition in verfe; while we clafs him in point of time as the laft poet of the age, we muft exalt him to the firft rank for the harmony and power of his numbers. He tranflated the eclogues of Virgil, applying the circumftances to the events of Ferdinand and Ifabel, in whofe praife he wrote his poem of

Triumfo

Triumfo de la fama, and his *Arte de poefia Caftellana* in profe, dedicated to the prince Don John, all which he completed, between the age of fourteen and twenty-five, as appears from the collection of his works printed at Saragoffa, in 1516.

The Caftilian mufe now began to affume a loftier flight.   Juan de Mena introduced an elegance of expreffion, George Manrique and his nephew (*a*) polifhed her ftyle, and em-

(*a*) George Manrique the nephew, was fon of Roderic Count of Paredes, and wrote an elegy on the death of his father, printed at Madrid, with a gloffary, in 1632, in 8vo, along with the *Coplas* of *Mingo Revulgo*, the moral proverbs of the marquis of Santillana, and other fugitive pieces.——The moral pieces of George Manrique, the uncle, were printed at Antwerp in 1594, with a comment by Francifco Guzman.

bellifhed

bellished it with more easy rhyme. The marquis of Santillana disembarrassed her from the fetters of couplets, and made her acquainted with the versification of the Provenzals and Italians. Finally, Juan de la Encina shewed her to be equal to the powers of the drama, following the example of the marquis of Villena. in translating the latin poets, and. in laying down precepts for the art,. which was as much as could be expected at that time.----Besides the *Cancionero* of Baena, a further *Cancionero general* was compiled by Hernan del Castillo, including all the poets from Juan de Mena down to the editor, and has gone through several editions, the third was at Seville in 1535, and another at Antwerp, in 1573.

LETTER

LETTER XI.

*The third period, or golden age of Spanish poetry,
in the 16th century.*

MADRID, 23d July, 1778.

I Went laſt night to take leave of ſome acquaintance previous to my departure for St. Ildefonſo, and ſpent the evening in a moſt agreeable party, at one of thoſe private aſſemblies, that go by the name of *Tertulias,* but from whence they have derived this appellation I can not inform you.---In many families theſe little parties are held every evening, and conſiſt of a number of ſelect friends, who enliven this friendly ſociety.

As

As foon as the company begins to affemble, they divide into different apartments ; refrefhments are immediately diftributed, confifting of fherbets, fweetmeats, and chocolate : a chearful and lively converfation is fupported on a variety of pleafing fubjeĉts, in which the prelate, the foldier, and the civilian, come in for a fhare, and the ladies contribute their part. In another apartment a more grave fet are amufed with cards, while a few gallant knights, with the crimfon infignia of chivalry on their breafts, divide themfelves , amongft the fair lifteners, and the amorous glance is enlivened by fparkling eyes and every expreffion of feature :—while one echoes the foft murmurs of love, a delicate finger

founds

founds the guitarre, and adds to its
harmony with a fong.—Each party
is happy, no tirefome ceremony in-
terrupts their felicity, the very idea
of jealoufy is ftruck out of the rubric:
wit and good humour are the principal purfuits, added to a chearful
mind, unbent with every focial attribute :—no plodding about politics
or the debts of the nation.---Happy
moments thus glide away imperceptibly, till the ufual hour comes, and
then every one retires in filence,
pleafed and contented !----Amongft a
variety of entertaining fubjects that are
occafionally difcuffed in this entertaining junto, they happened laft night
to fpeak of the golden age of poetry
in Spain, which was agreed upon, to
have taken place in the fixteenth century,

GARCILASO
DE LA VEGA.

tury, with the re-eſtabliſhment of letters in that kingdom, when a new field was opened to the muſes, who, baniſhed from the Eaſt, liſtened to the few Spaniards who courted them, and accepted of their addreſſes; at the time that a true taſte was reviving in Italy, under the influence of Sannazar, Bembo, and Arioſto, and the muſes recovering from that drooping ſtate they had fallen into at the death of Petrarch. The firſt promoters of this brilliant revolution in Spain, were Juan Boſcan, Garcilaſo de la Vega, the great Don Diego de Mendoza, Gutierre de Cetinia, and Don Lewis de Haro, who were followed by Franciſco Saa de Miranda, Pedro de Padilla, Gregorio Hernandez de Velaſco and others; who, beſides the Italian

rhyme,

rhyme, adorned their own language
with the further embellifhments re-
quired by the mufes, fuch as lively invention, graceful ftyle, purity of diction, and dignity of fentiment, equal
to elevated fubjects: to fhew, however,
the foibles of the human mind, with
the baneful effect of envy, when genius makes a new effort ; a fet of men
was not wanting, who looked with a
jealous eye on the verfification of the
Italians ; and fuch is the effect of prejudice, that it even worked upon the
moft ingenuous minds.   Bofcan acknowledges, that he attempted to introduce the new metre, at the perfua-
fion of Navagero, the Venetian ambaffador at the court of Charles the
5th, and he happily fucceeded, having compofed various fonnets and
                              paftorals,

paſtorals, in the Italian metre, which met with great acceptation, notwithſtanding the other party endeavoured to leſſen their merit, by calling ſuch poets by the name of *Petrarquiſts*. Boſcan tranſlated the fable of Leander and Hero from the Greek of Muſeus and a tragedy of Euripides, which ſerved to poliſh the ſtyle of his contemporary and friend Garcilaſo de la Vega. Boſcan further improved his mind by travel in Germany and Italy, in the ſervice of the emperor Charles, reaping the ſame advantages as Chaucer had done before him with us, and may be truly ſaid to be the Petrarch of Spain.

The great Don Diego de Mendoza merits a more particular inyeſtiga-

M

tion

tion from his exalted character as a poet, a foldier, and a flatefman. This illuftrious perfonage was of the noble houfe of Mendoza, being fon of Don Ignacio Lopez de Mendoza, fecond count of Tendilla, and marquis of Mondejar. Our poet was born in Granada, about the year 1500, and educated in the univerfity of Salamanca, where he applied himfelf clofely to the latin, greek, hebrew, and arabic languages. Befides the advantages of his high birth, he enjoyed thofe of court favour, and was honoured with the moft eminent dignities; for he was a *Commandeur* of the order of Alcantara, counfellor of ftate to the emperor Charles, and his ambaffador at Venice and at Rome, as well as at the famous Council of

Trent,

Trent, where he made a conspicuous figure. His long residence in Italy, added to his natural genius, gave him every opportunity of improvement, insomuch that he was reckoned one of the politest scholars, and most accomplished gentlemen of his time. He is said to have had a most forbidding aspect, added to a peculiar severity of temper, which was of great prejudice to him when he was governor of Sienna; he seems to have conveyed it to his verse, which is in general harsh, for he faintly imitated the manner of Boscan, and still retained the languid expression of old times, which he was not able to conquer, notwithstanding his frequent communication with the most celebrated poets of Italy. Whilst a stu-

M 2

dent

dent at the univerſity of Salamanca, he writ that little piece called *the life of Lazarillo de Tormes*, which was ſoon after tranſlated into Italian, and alſo into Engliſh : the great author little thought at that time, that his performance would ever ſerve to grace the ſtalls of Moorfields.——But this *en paſſant*, for he makes a conſiderable figure as an hiſtorian in his *Civil wars of Granada*, wherein he alſo ſpeaks as a contemporary, as his nephew the marquis of Mondejar, was the general, under whoſe command all thoſe great actions were performed. —— It is difficult to beſtow praiſes equal to the elegance of this claſſical performance, in which the beauty of ſtyle is ſo great, and the ſentiment every where ſo nobly ſup-

ported,

ported, that he rivals Salluſt and Tacitus; while as a ſoldier he has the correctneſs and temper of Cæſar, and may be ſaid to unite in the higheſt degree the character of a fine gentleman, and an experienced commander.---Many pieces of his, written with much freedom, ſtill remain in manuſcript in private hands, and in the grand duke's library at Florence. His other poems were printed, with the following title, *Obras del inſigne Cavallero Don Diego de Mendoza en Madrid*, 1610.----His fine library he bequeathed to Philip the 2d, and it ſerves as one of the principal ornaments of the eſcurial (*a*).

(*a*) The compiler of the new Spaniſh Parnaſſus, ſpeaking of Don Diego Mendoza, and of his having been ambaſſador in England, acknowledges he can-

 Another

Another valiant foldier now occurs, who diftinguifhed himfelf as a poet, and joined with Don Diego de Mendoza in introducing the metre of Petrarch, and polifhing the language of his own country. This was Garci-

not difcover at what time; which makes me think he miftook him for his brother, Don Bernardino de Mendoza, who was ambaffador in England in queen Elizabeth's time, and on her being informed that he had been concerned in all the cabals that Throcmorton and others had contrived againft her perfon and ftate, fhe caufed him to be fharply reprimanded by the council, who commanded him to depart the realm, which he not doing, they fent him on board captain Hawkins's veffel, who landed him at Calais, and Sir William Wade was fent to complain of Mendoza, and juftify the neceffity of the ftep; but Philip was fo offended, he would not fee him, and referred him to his council, on which Sir William quitted Spain, faying his orders were to addrefs himfelf to the king, and fince he would not admit him, he had then nothing more to do in the kingdom.——*Winquefort.*

lafo

lafo de la Vega, born at Toledo in 1503, knight of the order of Alcantara, and fon of Garcilafo de la Vega, ambaffador from the catholic king at the court of Rome, fon of Hernan Perez de Guzman, a celebrated poet. Garcilafo diftinguifhed himfelf early as a military man in the armies of Charles the fifth, particularly at the fiege of Tunis, where he was wounded in the face and in the arm. He attended the emperor in Piedmont, having eleven companies of infantry under his command, and was mortally wounded at the ftorming of a tower near Frejus, being only thirty-three years old, at which the emperor was fo irritated, that all the peafants who defended it, were put to the fword. Thus fell, in the

prime

prime of life, a gallant foldier and an accomplifhed genius, who had greatly improved the poetry of Spain by po-lifhing its numbers, and introducing the melody and harmony of the Ita-lian verfification, with which he had been early acquainted, as well as with the principal Italian poets of his time, fo that he has juftly been ftiled *The Prince of Spanifh poets*, having with his friend Bofcan brought the Spanifh poetry to its higheft perfec-tion.——Still the national pride of Don Chriftoval de Caftillejo, endeavoured to oppofe the progrefs of harmony and poetical numbers, and though he was at Vienna as fecretary to prince Ferdinand, afterwards emperor; he ftill inveighed againft his country-men, particularly in a fatyrical piece

" againft

" againſt thoſe who quitted the Spaniſh metre to adopt the Italian :" and
in a poem intitled *Petrarquiſtas*, he in-
troduces Juan de Mena, George Manrique, Garci Sanchez, Cartagena, and
Torres Naharro, as followers of the
Spaniſh metre, in oppoſition to Boſcan, Garcilaſo, Don Luis de Haro, and
Don Diego Mendoza, accuſing this
laſt of having made uſe of verſe with
leaden feet.

You will find neverthelefs in the
poets of this age, a ſoftneſs and fluency unknown to their predeceſſors ;
Hernandez diſtinguiſhed himſelf by
his tranſlation of the Æneis of Virgil, and his firſt and fourth ec-
logue, as alfo the poem of Sannazzar
de partu virginis. Juan de Guzman
likewiſe

likewife tranflated the Georgics of Virgil with the greateft fuccefs, which were printed at Salamanca in 1586.

Lope de Rueda, a celebrated actor, now began to give fome form to the Spanifh ftage, being alfo a principal performer of his own compofitions, which were publifhed after his death, by Juan Timoneda ; he was followed by Bartholome de Torre Naharro, another writer for the ftage, whofe comedies and other poems were publifhed by himfelf, under the whimfical name of *Propaladia*: Juan de la Cueva was the next in fucceffion to Naharro, who adorned the dramatic mufe, as Don Alonfo de Ercilla did the epic.

Fernando

Fernando de Herrera, by a singular caprice, acquired the firname of *Divine* from the fire and energy of his verfe, though he was furpaffed in facility of rhyme by Don Eftevan Manuel de Villegas, who admirably enriched his own language with all the graces of the Latin fapphics, Hexameters and Pentameters, uniting the wit of Horace, the graces of Anacreon, the freedom and elegance of Tibullus, with the politenefs of Propertius, and the natural turn of Theocritus. His poems were publifhed under the title of *Eroticas.* He alfo tranflated Boetius, in a manner equal to his great reputation.

The perfecuted Father Lewis de Leon may juftly be ftiled one of the

principal

principal favourites of the mufes in this polite age, imitating Pindar, Horace, Virgil and Tibullus, as well as Petrarch and Bembo.---His elegant verfions of the facred writings drew on him an unjuft and fevere perfecution from his rivals, and after long and cruel fufferings in the dark prifons of the inquifition, he came out with honour and triumph, to the confufion and difgrace of his enemies! Next to him we muft place the two brothers of the name of Argenfola, who equally claim the title of the Horace of Spain, and have not fince been equalled.

We muft alfo write with golden letters in the temple of fame, a celebrated ftatefman, Gonzalo Perez, fe-

cretary

cretary of ſtate to Philip the ſecond, and father·to the unfortunate Antonio Perez, ſecretary to Philip, as his father had been, and whoſe melancholy ſtory is well known : Having had the good fortune to eſcape from Philip, he finiſhed his days in obſcurity, in France, under the protection of Henry the 4th. With the permiſſion of queen Elizabeth, he went, for a little time, to England, and was in correſpondence with Eſſex and other perſons of that time.---But to return to his father Gonzalo, he diſtinguiſhed himſelf as a poet by an elegant tranſlation of the Odyſſey of Homer, in blank verſe, in which attempt he ſtood unrivalled till the Britiſh muſe, jealous of a foreign bard, diſputed with him the honour of excelling

celling in fo noble a career.----As for Chriftoval de Mefa, he faintly clofes the expiring æra, and though a fcholar of Taffo, with whom he lived five years in Rome, he remained far behind him, and unequal to epic poetry: fome of his performances are tolerable, fuch as the fable of Narciffus, from Ovid, his imitation of the *Beatus Iile* of Horace, a poetical compendium of the art of poetry, and fome paftorals.----After this laft effort, we muft now view the Spanifh mufe like a ftately tree, arrived at its ultimate period of improvement, and gently bending its head to the all powerful influence of time, gradually declining with the progeny of Philip the 2d, who, after a long reign, expired in the Efcurial, overwhelm-

ed

ed with difeafe, in the moſt excru-
ciating pains, and devoured by vermin. The mufes wept, forefeeing the
decline of the Philips, and clofed the
brightneſs of their days with the century! One of the laſt writers who
fupported this tottering fabric, was
the Count de Rebolledo, a gentleman of diſtinguiſhed talents, and a
foldier of great intrepidity. He ferved firſt in the marine department,
under Don Pedro de Leyva, and having the command of a galley, gave
proofs of the utmoſt bravery againſt
the Turks: he afterwards ferved in
Flanders with equal reputation as a
colonel of horfe, and was employed
as a miniſter to the imperial court on
bufineſs of great moment; and Ferdinand the 2d, being at the diet of Ra-
tiſbonne,

tisbonne, was so pleased with his conduct and prudence, though at that
time only thirty-six years of age, that
he conferred on him the dignity of a
Count of the sacred Roman Empire.
----He was afterwards minister ple-
nipotentiary in Denmark, after which
he returned to Madrid and was
of the council of war, and died in
his eightieth year, universally regretted.----His works were printed at
Copenhagen and Antwerp; many of
his poems are dedicated to Chris-
tina Queen of Sweden; his *Selva
Danica* to Sophia Amelia Queen of
Denmark, and his *Selva Militar y Po-
litica* to his own sovereign, Philip the
4th, from whom there are sixty-eight
original letters extant, written to him
from 1648 to 61, many of the king's

own

own hand, while in Denmark; seven from the cardinal Infant Don Ferdinand, and other illuftrious perfonages.

Many poets however fupported the fpirit of the golden age; fuch as Vicente Efpinel, Don Luis de Ulloa, Pedro de Efpinofa, Don Francifco Quevedo, Don Juan de Jauregui, Solis the hiftorian and others, who like falling leaves announced the long winter that was to follow. The name of Quevedo is well known to you, and his *vifions* which have been tranflated into Englifh; his genius was fuch that neither the perfecutions he fuffered from his enemies, or other mortifications, could damp his bold mafculine fpirit, or the keennefs of his fatire; befides his merit as a poet

N   he

he was well verfed in the oriental languages and of great erudition.--- His poems appeared under the feign-ed name of the Bachelor Francifco de la Torre. When the Duke of Of-funa was viceroy of Naples, he was employed in feveral commiffions of confequence amongft the Italian ftates, and had the addrefs to go to Venice, on a particular object, difguifed as a mendicant. The viceroy fent him to court, acknowledging his great fer-vices, for which he was made a knight of St. James.—When the duke's in-tereft and favour declined, he came in for his fhare of difgrace, and was three years in confinement, afflicted with illnefs, but nothing appearing againft him, he was fet at liberty. Dif-gufted with the ficklenefs of court fa-

vour,

vour and attendance on the great, he refused several employments that were offered him, as well in the miniflry, as the embaffy to Genoa; and retired to his own feat, where he gave himfelf up intirely to literary purfuits. At the age of fifty-four, he entered into the ftate of matrimony, with Dona Efperanza de Aragon, a lady of rank, whom he foon had the misfortune to lofe, finding no other alleviation than fuch as arofe from his philofophical difpofition. But the envenomed fhafts of envy ftill reached him in his folitude; -----on a falfe accufation of being author of an infamous libel, he was arrefted in the night, put in clofe confinement, and his eftate fequeftered. In this fituation he laboured under various

N 2　　　　　difeafes

diseases with acute pain of body and mind; his patrimony seized, and himself supported by charity! Under this distress he wrote that elegant and pathetic letter to the prime minister *Olivarez*, which procured him his enlargement: the case was enquired into, and the calumny, as well as its author, discovered. He once more returned to court to recover his estate, which had suffered various depredations, but this ungrateful theatre he soon abandoned, and retired to his country seat, overwhelmed with illness, the consequence of his cruel imprisonment; all which he bore with manly fortitude, and finished his days with exemplary and christian resignation in the 65th year of his age, in 1645. His person was engaging, his complexion

complexion fair, and great expreffion,
in his countenance; but from conti-
nual fludy, his eyes were fo weakened,
that he conftantly wore fpectacles.—
Such was Quevedo, one of the greateft fcholars and eminent poets of his
time, whofe youth was fpent in the
fervice of his country in Italy, where
he diftinguifhed himfelf with the utmoft fagacity and prudence.---To give
you an idea of his extenfive knowledge and profound erudition, I own.
myfelf at a lofs, much lefs to fpeak of
his numerous though excellent writings.---His moral difcourfes prove
his found doctrine and religious fentiments, while his literary pieces dif-
play his infinite judgment and refined tafle.---His great knowledge of
Hebrew is apparent from the report

of the hiftorian Mariana to the king, requefting that Quevedo might revife the new edition of the bible of Arias Montanus. His tranflations of Epictetus and Phocylides, with his imitations of Anacreon and other Greek authors, fhew how well he was verfed in that language : That he was a Latin fcholar, his conftant correfpondence, from the age of twenty, with Lipfius, Chifflet, and Scioppius, will fufficiently illuftrate.—As a poet he excelled both in the ferious and burlefque ftyle, and was fingularly happy in that particular turn we have fince admired in Butler and Swift. His library, which confifted of about five thoufand volumes, was reduced, at his death, to about two thoufand, and is preferved in the convent of St. Martin,

Martin, at Madrid.---Were I to en-
large further, refpecting this great
man, I fhould eafily fill a moderate
volume.---But it is time to proceed,
before we behold the fetting fun, and a
mift arife over the poetical horizon,
which various incidents have obfcured and greatly deprived of its original luftre.

The *Diana Enamorada* of Gil Polo,
an elegant poet in the fixteenth century, was reprinted in London, in
1739, under the infpection of Pedro
de Pineda.---Jauregui tranflated Lucan, but not with that fuccefs as he
did the *Aminta* of Taffo. I clofe the
golden age with the immortal Miguel
de Cervantes ;---like another Homer,
many cities contended for his birth,

 and

and his tranfcendant merit you are
well acquainted with.   In his poem
intitled *A Voyage to Parnaffus*, he has
delineated the characters of the poets of his time.---he equally fhines
as a dramatic writer, but every thing
of his is totally eclipfed by his incom-
parable romance of *Don Quixote*, which,
alone crowns his temples with never
fading laurels.

Thus ended the golden age of the
Spanifh mufe, whofe period of glory was fhort, though the attempt to
fecure its duration feemed to promife
a more lafting reign, if a clofe imitation of the antients, and the precepts of thofe great mafters, Ariftotle
and Horace, could have fecured to
them the prize; or fome invifible
caufe

caufe had not with hafty ftrides brought on its decline : but before I fpeak of this laft period, I tranf-mit you an ode of Horace in Spa-nifh, Italian, and Englifh, from whence you may form a comparative judgment of the energy and powers of each language. I have fubjoined a few fpecimens of hexameters, fapphics, adonics, and epigrams, which will give you fome idea of the harmony of Spanifh numbers in its moft im-proved ftate.

Adieu !

ODE

ODE XXIII.

Ad Fuscum Aristium.

INTEGER vitæ scelerisque purus
Non eget mauri Jaculis, neque arcu
Nec venenatis gravida sagittis,
Fusce pharetra.

Sive per syrtes iter æstuosas,
Sive facturus per inhospitalem
Caucasum, vel quæ loca fabulosus
Lambit Hydaspes.

Namque me sylva lupus in Sabina,
Dum meam canto Lalagen, et ultra
Terminum curis vagor expeditus,
Fugit inermem.

Quale portentum neque militaris
Daunia in latis alit esculetis:
Nec Jubæ tellus generat, leonum,
Arida nutrix.

Pone me pigris ubi nulla campis
Arbor æstiva recreatur aura;
Quod latus mundi nebulæ, malusque
Jupiter urget.

Pone sub curru nimium propinqui
Solis, in terra domibus negata:
Dulce ridentem Lalagen amabo,
Dulce loquentem.

In

In SPANISH.

The same by Don Antonio de Solis, author of the history of the conquest of Mexico.

NO ha menester defenderse
   Con dardos arrojadizos
Quien vive con entereza,
Y camina sin delito.

Sobrale el arco y la aljaba,
Con el embrion maligno
De venenas factas
Que anaden malicia al tiro.

O camine por las sirtas
Abrasadas del estio,
O el Caucaso inhabitable
Penetre con pie sencillo.

O bien pise los horrores
De los formidables riscos,
Que undoso lame el Hydafpes
Antes de befar el Indo.

Que entre los mayores riesgos
Camina bien defendido
El que va con la innocencia
Que es virtud sin enemiga.

N. B. *The last strophe of Horace seems to have been
omitted by the Spanish poet.*

In

In ITALIAN.

By Dr. Maffei, of Leghorn, in his translation of
Horace, dedicated to Sir John Dick, Bart.
his Majesty's Consul at Leghorn, and knight
of St. Anne of Russia.

CHI e giusto, e puro
　　Di diletti ha il petto,
Fusco non cerca,
Mauri dardi, o l'arco
Ne la faretra
Piena di saette
Avvelenate:
O muova i passi
Per le sirti ardenti
O sia che debba
Valicare il monte
Caucaso, o i luogi
Dove favuloso
Scorre l'Idaspe.
Poiche la mia
Lalage cantando
Mentre minoltro
Nel Sabino bosco,
Scevro di cure

Disarmato,

In ENGLISH,

By Wentworth Dillon Earl of Roscommon.

VIRTUE, dear friend! needs no defence,
  The sureſt guard is innocence;
None knew 'till guilt created fear
What darts or poiſoned arrows were!

Integrity undaunted goes
Through Lybian ſands or Scythian ſnows,
Or where Hydaſpes' wealthy tide
Pays tribute to the Perſian pride.

For as by am'rous thoughts betray'd
Careleſs in Sabin woods I ſtray'd,
A griſly foaming wolf unfed,
Met me unarm'd, yet trembling fled.

No beaſt of more portentous ſize,
In the Hercinian foreſt lies,
None fiercer in Numidia bred,
With Carthage were in triumph led.

Set me in the remoteſt place,
That Neptune's frozen arms embrace,

Where

Difarmato, e folo,
Me fuge un lupo,
Qual la guerriera
Daunia militare
Moftro non nutre
Nelle vafte felve,
Ne la Numidia
Forma di leon
Arida madre
Nei pigri campi,
Dove pianta eftiva
Giammai leggiero
Zeffiro recrea
Pommi, cui nebbia,
Ed il procellofo
Giove molefta:
O fotto il carro
Pommi del vicino
Sole, nei luooghi
Vedovi di tetti,
Dolce ridente
Lalage amerò
Dolce parlante.

Where angry Jove did never spare
One breath of kind and temp'rate air.

Set me where on some pathless plain
The swarthy Africans complain,
To see the chariot of the sun
So near their scorching country run.

The burning zone, the frozen isles
Shall hear me sing of Celia's smiles:
All cold, but in her breast I will despise;
And dare all heat! but that in Celia's eyes,

SPECIMEN

SPECIMEN of HEXAMETERS,

By Don Eſtevan Manuel de Villegas.

EGLOGA.

LICIDAS Coridon, y Coridon el amante de Filis,
　Paſtor el uno de cabras, el otro de blancas ovejas,
Ambos a dos tiernos, mozos ambos, arcades ambos,
Viendo que los rayos del ſol fatigaban al orbe,
Y que vibrando fuego feroz la canicula ladra,
Al puro criſtal, que cria la fuente ſonora,
Llevedos del ſon alegre de ſu blando ſuſurro,
Las plantas veloces mueven, los paſos animan,
Y al tronco de un verde enebro ſe ſientan amigos.

SAPPHICS.

By the ſame band.

DULCE vecino de la verde ſelva,
　Hueſped eterno del abril florido,
Vital aliento de la madre Venus,
　　　　　Zephiro blando.

Si de mis anſias el amor ſupiſte;
Tu, que las quejas de mi voz llevaſte,
Oye: no temas, y a mi ninfa dile,
　　　　　Dile, que muero.

Filis

Filis un tiempo mi dolor fabia,
Filis un tiempo mi dolor lloraba,
Quifome un tiempo; mas agora temo,
     Temo fus iras.

Afi los diofes con amor paterno,
Afi los cielos con amor benigno,
Nieguen al tiempo, que feliz volares,
     Nieve a la tierra.

Jamás el pefo de la nube parda,
Quando amanece la elevada cumbre,
Torque tus hombros, ni fu mal granizo.
     Hiera tus alas.

ADONICS.

By Geronimo Bermudez.

O! Corazones
  Mas que de tigres!
O! manos crudas
Mas que de fieras,
Como pudiftes
Tan innocente,
Tan apurada
   O   Sangre

Sangre verter!
Ay! que su grito,
O Lusitania,
Patria mia,
Ay que su grito
Desde la tierra
Rompe los cielos,
Rompe las nnbes,
Rompe los ayres,
Trae las llamas
Del zelo vivo,
Trae los rayos
Del vivo fuego
Que purifica
Toda la tierra
Contaminada
De la crueza
Que cometiste!
Trae la vara,
Trae el azote,
Trae la peste,
Trae la furia
Que te castiga
Sin piedad.
Etc. - - - - - -

ANACRE-

ANACREONTIC ODE,

By Don Estevan Manuel de Villegas.

YO vi sobre un tomillo
  Quexarse un paxarillo
Viendo su nido amado,
De quien era caudillo,
De un labrador robado.
Vile tan congojado
Por tal atrevimiento
Dar mil quexas al viento,
Para que al cielo santo
Lleve su tierno llanto,
Lleve su triste acento.
Ya con triste harmonia,
Es forzando el intento,
Mil quexas repetia:
Ya cansado callaba:
Y al nuevo sentimiento
Ya sonoro volvia.
Ya circular volaba:
Ya rastrero corria:
Ya, pues, de rama en rama

Al

Al ruſtico ſeguia ;
Y ſaltando en la grama,
Parece que decia :
Dame, ruſtico fiero,
Mi dulce compania :
Y que le reſpondia
El ruſtico : *no quiero.*

PINDARIC ODE,

By Father Lewis de Leon.

EL agua es bien precioſo,
  Y entre el rico teſoro,
Como el ardiente fuego en noche eſcura
Anſi relumbra el oro.
Mas, alma ſi es ſabroſo
Cantar de las contiendas la ventura,
Anſi como en la altura
No hay rayo mas luciente,
Que el ſol, que rey del dia.
Por todo el yermo cielo ſe demueſtra ;
Anſi es mas excelente
La olimpica porfia
De todas las que canta la voz nueſtra :
Materia abundante,
Donde todo elegante

Ingenio

Ingenio alza la voz, ora cantando
De Rea, y de Saturno el engendrado,
Y Juntamente entrando
Al techo de Hieron alto preciado.

- - - - - - - - - - - -
- - - - - - - - - - - -

C A N C I O N.

*By Garcilaſo de la Vega, dedicated to Violante
Sanſeverino, daughter to the Duke de Soma, in
Naples.*

SI de mi baja lira
   Tanto pudieſe el ſon, que un momento
Aplicaſe la ira
Del animoſo vento,
Y la furia del mar, y el movimiento;
Y en aſperas montanas,
Con el ſuave canto enternecieſe
Las fieras animales,
Los arboles movieſe,
Y al ſon confuſamente los truxeſe:
No pienſes que cantando
Seria de mi, hermoſa flor de gnido,
El fiero Marte ayrado,
A muerte convertido,
De polvo, y ſangre, y de ſudor tenido:

O 3

Ni

Ni aquellos capitanes,
En la sublime rueda colocados,
Por quien los alemanes
El fiero cuello atados,
Y los franceses van domesticados.

EPIGRAM.

By Baltazar del Alcazar.

MAGDALENA me picó
   Con un alfiler un dedo:
Dije la : picado quedo,
Pero ya lo estaba yo,
Riose, y con su cordura
Acudió al remedio presto :
Chupóme el dedo, y con esto
Sané de la picadura.

EPIGRAM.

*By Lope de Vega on Charles Prince of Wales,
when he went to Madrid to court the In-
fanta of Spain.*

CARLOS Stuardo soy
   Que siendo *Amor,* mi guia
Al cielo de España voy
Por ver mi estrella *Maria !*

LETTER XII.

Fourth period and decline of Spanish Poetry in the seventeenth century.

St. ILDEFONSO, 26th July, 1778.

LIKE another Don Quixote, I sallied forth from Madrid, on one of the hotteſt days in July, and having traverſed a bleak country and climbed ſteep and almoſt perpendicular mountains, I at laſt reached, with a good deal of labour, the royal ſeat of St. Ildefonſo, in a wild and barren ſituation, where, for the ſake of the cool air that conſtantly reigns here, Philip the 5th thought fit to diſplay his magnificence, by converting one of the moſt barren

O 4   ſpots

ſpots in nature into a royal villa, where the laviſh expence of Ver-ſailles was to be renewed, and the French taſte of gardening exhibited, with the formal lines of ſtiff deſign and antiquated ſymetry. Nature, it is true, aſſiſted them with the moſt clear and limpid water, which they have made uſe of to advantage ; ſhade being here an object of principal luxury, the gardens have the ap-pearance of a perfect paradiſe, on leaving the ſultry air of Madrid. But notwithſtanding this contraſt, it is here ſo piercing at night, and its tranſitions ſo ſudden as to be of-ten productive of dangerous effects on the conſtitution; for while you paſs the day agreeably, dreſſed in ſilk, a Ruſſian fur is acceptable at night.

Though

Though every effort is made in these gardens, in the midst of snowy mountains, to support vegetation, and force a smile on nature, yet every thing looks languid; and instead of the blooming aspect of summer, it rather puts me in mind of the subject I proposed continuing in my last letter, when having traced the Spanish muse in the bright days of splendour, I come now to descant upon her withered bays, like the puny products of St. Ildefonso, that have the colour and resemblance of youth, but nothing of its juvenile vigour and strength.—Thus it happened to the Spanish muse in the seventeenth century, to which the false taste that had already crept in amongst the Italians contributed not

a little,

a little, and ferved to haften their decline; even the Tufcan mufe, after foaring to the higheft pinnacle of glory, infenfibly began to lofe her priftine comelinefs under the tuition of Marini and his pupils, who by a ftrain of falfe fimilies and extravagant conceits, ftripped the mufes of their natural graces. The Spaniards foon catched the contagion in the feeble condition they were in, and Lorenzo Gracian, fome of whofe works have been tranflated into Englifh, further eftablifhed this falfe tafte, which he attempted to methodize in a formal effay, entitled *de Agudeza y arte de Ingenio*; by which means the pleafing elegance of nature was disfigured by a combination of pedants, who lofing fight of every beautiful idea, con-

temning

temning at the same time, the rules
of art, made way for their infipid va-,
garies.---Thefe unmerciful defpoilers .
may be claffed under three heads in
Spain ; the firft violated all the laws
of the drama, and introduced innu-,
merable defects on the, ftage; which
have never been eradicated: of thefe,
Chriftoval de Virues, Lope de Vega,
and Montalban, were the principal.
leaders, and were followed by Calderon, Salazar, Candamo, Zamora, and
others, who to the moft glaring im-
proprieties, fuperadded a ridiculous
bombaft and affectation of language,
which became fuperlatively intolera-
ble and abfurd.----The fecond clafs
confifted of thofe who in imitation of
the Italians and their unnatural *Con-*
celli, introduced fuch an extravagant

profufion

profufion of falfe fentiment, equivo-
cal expreffion, and fwollen periods,
as recalled to mind thofe ancient
times, when fuch men had been fo
feverely handled by Horace ; and
not content with doing fo much in-
jury to the drama, they further extended it to lyric compofitions.---The
third clafs was diftinguifhed by the
pedantic appellation of *Cultos*, " or
refined," which comprehended a fet
of puritans, who out of falfe zeal for
the chaftity of the mufes, endeavoured to introduce a greater purity
of diction, but by their awkward
and ignorant prefumption, fubfti-
tuted obfcure and unknown expreffions to a new and turgid dialect. At
the head of thefe was the poet Luis
de Gongora, the count de Villame-
diana,

diana, with others of lefs note, who contributed to diffufe an univerfal bad tafte, and difcredit the mufes, fapping the very foundations of their temple, and pointing their fhafts againft the few remnants of beauty and eloquence in every branch of literature: to fuch a low ftate was true genius reduced by thefe vandals, that the greateft applaufes were given to vile punfters and minftrels, and every retailer of falfe wit, under the denomination of *Difcreciones*, who in a former age would have been hiffed off the ftage with the moft fovereign contempt.

While an univerfal langour thus pervaded every mind, the royal ftem partook of a fimilar decline of nature.

ture.   The progeny of the great emperor Charles now drew near to its
laſt gaſp.   whatever may have been
the cauſe, the muſes gradually
drooped with the empire of theſe
monarchs, and in conjunction with
the diſmembered dominions of the
Philips, expired under the feeble
Charles the ſecond, who leaving no
iſſue, a prince of the houſe of Bourbon aſcended the throne of Spain.—
The national dreſs of the Spaniard,
as well as his character, were altered;
his ſable garment was changed for
the gay and effeminate modes of
Verſailles; Spaniſh gravity was put
out of countenance, and he was deprived of his darling whiſkers; as the
ſavage Ruſſians much about the ſame
time

time had been defpoiled of their beards (a).--Perhaps you are unacquainted with the importance of whifkers at that time in Spain and Portugal : It is told of Don Joam de

(a) When the emperor Charles's german foldiers quarrelled with their Spanifh comrades, they ufed to fwear in german *By Got*, laying hold of their whifkers; from whence the Spaniards miftaking the meaning of the word, have called whifkers ever fince by the name of *Bigotes*, though the original word is *Moftacho*, from the Greek word μυσαξ the upper lip.--Whifkers and beards were points of great confequence in Spain in thofe days and any infult offered to them was not to be borne with, even after death by the *Cid*, as the grave Cobarruvias tells us, *It was faid*, that a Jew having pulled him by the beard on his tomb, out of contempt, God permitted that the figure of this champion fhould extend its marble hand to its fword, and draw it one third out of the fcabbard; on which the affrighted Jew fcreamed out, which brought people together, who related the ftory, and fome *faid* it canfed the Jew to become a Chriftian '

Caftro,

Caftro, a Portugueze viceroy in India, that being in great want of money, and defirous to borrow a large fum in that country, he pawned one of his whifkers, as the moft facred pledge he could think of; which he afterwards honourably redeemed: in which he acted with more punctilio than that famous Spanifh hero the *Cid*, who obtaining a fum of money of a jew on his plate, inftead of fending it to his houfe, ordered only a cheft of fand;—though he afterwards made reftitution in his will.

Adieu.—My next will be from the Efcurial, where I am going to fpend a few days, and then prepare matters for my departure for England.

LETTER

LETTER XIII.

Remarks made in the library of the Escurial, on Spanish commentators, poetical translations of greek and latin classics, and italian authors.

ESCURIAL, August 2d, 1778.

I HAVE taken this opportunity to come to the Escurial in order to view this grand edifice more at leisure, when the court is not here, and to indulge a few hours study and research in this very curious library, of which you have already heard so much, as well as of the famous building of the Escurial, the great work of the gloomy Philip the second, which cost him six millions of ducats. His long reign furnished him more-

P   over

over the pleasure of seeing it perfected, with the additional satisfaction of the whole having been compleated under the direction of two Spanish architects, John Baptist de Toledo, and his pupil Juan de Herrera; a structure of which you have of late seen so many accurate accounts, that it leaves me little to add on the subject, more than to inform you, that, as to the exaggeration of this building having eleven thousand windows, fourteen thousand doors, and eight hundred pillars, it is denied by their own writers, as well as what has been said of the tabernacle on the great altar being of porphyry, with eighteen pillars of agate, and being fourteen years making; also that the ceiling of the choir was painted by

Titian;

Titian : that the glafs windows were fixed in frames of filver gilt, and that the library contained an hundred thoufand volumes; all which are fabulous inventions, introduced by novel writers and book-makers, to amufe the credulous public in foreign countries.

The library may contain about thirty thoufand volumes, and may undoubtedly be efteemed as a very curious and valuable collection : I fpent a confiderable time there with great delight. It would be an herculean labour to attempt giving a feries of the numerous collections of Spanifh poets, commentators and tranflators, from the Greek, Latin and Italian poets, I mean to confine my-

felf

felf only to poetical books. The
moft antient collection of poems
is that made by Baena in the reign
of John the 2d, mentioned before;
which is in manufcript in this library,
and continued by Hernando del Caf-
tillo.---Lorenzo de Ayala publifhed
at Valencia, in 1588, another collection, entitled *Jardin de amadores*,
" The garden of lovers;" to which
may be added the *Romancero general*
of Miguel de Madrigal, in 1604,
that of Flores in Madrid in 1614,
and the firft part of the *Teforo de Di-
vina poefia* from various writers. Pedro de Efpinofa compiled the firft part
of the *flores de poetas iluftres de Efpana*,
printed at Valladolid in 1605, wherein the compiler alfo makes a confpicuous figure.

It

It was the misfortune of letters, at that time in Spain, to be
loaded with commentators, who
equally preſſed good and bad authors
into the ſervice, and burthened them
with the weight of their dullneſs; thoſe
who had not the temerity to attempt
the Greek and Latin claſſics, becauſe
they did not underſtand them, fell
without mercy on the works of their
countrymen, and ſome would comment upon their own works, which gave
birth to the moſt monſtrous productions. Even the learned Marquiſs de
Santillana commented upon his own
Proverbios; the poets Juan de Mena
and Garcilaſo de la Vega had numerous commentators; and the obſcure Gongora had three ſuch writers, who were ſo unſucceſsful that

P 3

they

they require another commentator for themselves.

The tranflations of poets in the Spanifh language are numerous, taken from Greek and Latin authors, as well as from the Provenzal, Italian, Portugueze, and latterly from the French. Gonzalo Perez tranflated the odyffey of Homer, and Chriftoval de Mefa the iliad, which laft is ftill in manufcript. The medea of Euripides was tranflated by Pedro Simon Abril in Barcelona, in 1599. Bofcan tranflated from the Greek poet Mufeus, as Lewis de Leon did from Pindar, and Villegas from Theocritus. Of Virgil there are feveral tranflations befides that of the Marquifs of Villena. Juan de la Encina tranfla-

ted

ted the eclogues in 1516, at Saragoffa, Juan de Guzman, a fcholar of the famous Sanctius Brocenfis, that is, Sanchez of Brozas in Eftremadura, tranflated the Georgics in blank verfe at Salamanca in 1586. Chriftoval de Mefa tranflated the æneis in octave rhymes in 1615, but that by Luis de Leon, publifhed by Quevedo at Madrid in 1631, is far fuperior, and may be confidered as an excellent performance.

The art of poetry of Horace has been excellently tranflated by Efpinel as well as by Luis de Zapata, printed in Spanifh verfe at Lifbon in 1592.

Ovid's metamorphofes have been tranflated into Spanifh by feve-

ral

ral hands, particularly by Philip Mey
at Tarragona in 1586, with great fuccefs, which fhews the tafte of Don
Antonio Aguftin archbifhop of Tarragona, who kept Mey in his palace
as a printer, whom he employed in
his own valuable and learned works.
This great prelate notwithftanding his
ferious occupations had a favourable
opinion of the mufes: He began a
poem in praife of the fountain of
Alcover, which he had obferved in a
vifitation of his diocefe, and directed
Mey to finifh it.——The epiftles of
Ovid were tranflated in blank verfe
by Don Francifco de Aldana a captain in the army under Philip II. but
when the author's brother Cofmo
printed his other poems at Madrid
in 1591, this work was fo fcarce that

he

he was obliged to omit it. Many other tranflations from the greek and latin claffics are to be found, and I have this moment received a new book on that fubject from Madrid, by Don Juan Antonio Pellicer of the king's library, who has juft publifhed an introductory effay to a future work, which is to comprehend all the learned Spaniards who have tranflated the fathers, philofophers, greek and latin hiftorians and poets (a).

The italian poets were introduced at an early period into Spain. It is

(a) Enfayo de una bibliotheca de Traductores Efpanoles donde fe da noticia de las traduciones que hay en Caftillano de la Sagrada Efcritura, Santos Padres, filofophos, hiftoriadores medicos, oradores, poetas, afi griegos como latinos; y de otros autores que han florecido antes de la invencion de la imprenta por Don Juan Antonio Pellicer y Saforcada, &c. Madrid, 1778.

fomewhat

fomewhat remarkable that all their great geniuffes owed their improvement to the italian fchool.   It was there that Mendoza, Bofçan, Garcilafo de la Vega, Quevedo, Ercilla, and many others formed their tafte, and when the Spaniards loft their dominions in Italy at the death of Charles II. it feems to have been the principal caufe of the decline of literature amongft them.

The learned Marquifs of Villena had at a very early period given a tranflation of Dante at the defire of the Marquifs of Santillana, and the fame poet was afterwards tranflated in verfe with notes by Don Pedro Fernandes de Villegas arcdeacon of Burgos,

gos, and printed in that city in 1515, at the end of which the 10th satire of Juvenal is added by the author's brother Geronimo de Villegas prior of Cuevas Rubias.—— The *Triomfi* of Petrarch was turned into Spanish verse and published at Medina del campo in 1554. The *Orlando furioso* of Ariosto was translated at Toledo in 1510 and again by Don Geronimo de Urrea, printed at Lyons in 1556. *The Tears of St. Peter* by Tansillo, an italian poet of the twelfth century, has been twice given in Spanish, first by Lewis Galvet de Montalvo, at Toledo, in 1587, and then by Don Juan de Sedeno. Tansillo having written a licentious poem in his youth, it was suppressed at Rome, and inserted in the *Index* of prohibited books,

books, which affected him so much,
that it occasioned this elegant poem
of the *Tears of St. Peter*, which the famous Malherbe has also translated
into French. Tansillo has been
sometimes compared to Petrarch.
The *Gierusalemme Liberata* of Tasso
has been translated into Spanish by
Juan de Sedeno at Madrid, in 1587.
—There are two translations of the
Pastor Fido of Guarini, the first by
Suarez de Figueroa, of Valencia, in
1609, the second by the fair hand
of a Lady, Dona Isabela de Correa,
and printed at Antwerp in 1694.
But to return to Tasso, Faria a Portugueze writer proves in his life of Camoens, that the poem of the Lusiad
is prior to Tasso, as the Lusiad was
published in 1572, and the first

edition

edition of the *Gierufalemme Liberata* appeared imperfect in 1581, and compleat at Venice in 1582, which is nine years later than the Lufiad; from whence it is evident the Portugueze had a correct epic poem before the Italians. Faria even goes further, and endeavours to fhew that Taffo has borrowed fome of his moft beautiful paffages from the Lufitanian bard: it is moreover fingular, that while Voltaire endeavours to depreciate the Lufiad with the feeming jealoufy of a rival, he extols fome paffages of the *Araucana*, a Spanifh poem by Don Alonfo de Ercilla, wherein the French poet compares the fpeech of the Indian chief *Colocòlo* to his people, with that of Neftor to Achilles and Agamemnon in the

firft

firſt book of the Iliad, and gives the ſuperiority to the Spaniard over Homer. You will of courſe be curious to hear ſomething further of ſuch a diſtinguiſhed writer. Don Alonſo de Ercilla, a gentleman of Biſcay, was a knight of the order of St. James, and gentleman of the bedchamber to the emperor Rodolph the 2d. He was brought up at court from his youth, having been page to the emperor Charles and Philip his ſon, whom he attended in all his expeditions to Italy, Flanders, Germany, and England. Being in London, when he heard that a rebellion had broken out in the town of *Arauco* in South America, he immediately quitted England and embarked for America, as a volunteer in

the

D. ALONSO
DE ERCILLA

the caufe of his country, where he diflinguifhed himfelf with extraordinary valour againft the Indians, writing by night the actions he had been witnefs of by day, and for want of other conveniencies, compofing his poem on fcraps of paper, or pieces of leather, taking up alternately the fword or the pen;----after many acts of heroifm, he had the good fortune to return to the court of his mafter, and produce a beautiful poem which was perfected at the age of twenty-nine; the firft part of which was printed in 1577, fo that he holds a diftinguifhed rank amongft the poets of the golden age, though I had not mentioned him before; as does alfo Don Francifco de Borja prince of Equilache, knight of

the

the golden fleece, and viceroy of Peru
till the death of Philip 'the 3d, in
1621, on receiving news of which,
he embarked for Spain, and retired
to Valencia, his native country, tho'
he went again to the court of Madrid,
where he died in his 80th year. In
his leifure hours, he principally devo-
ted himfelf to the mufes, and chiefly
excelled in lyric compofitions, infomuch that he has been claffed
amongft the nine mufes of Spain,
which, with himfelf confifted of Garcilafo de la Vega, Villegas, Quevedo,
the count de Rebolledo, the two Ar-
genfolas, Lewis de Leon, and Lope
de Vega.

I fay nothing to you of the fine
collection of Arabic manufcripts, in
the

the library of the Efcurial, many of which are curioufly painted and em-blazoned : Were I to fpeak to you of a fifter art, or had I the mufical talents of a Burney, I might give you a further defcription of a curi-ous book in this collection, being a treatife upon mufic, with defigns of upwards of thirty different mufical inftruments, which would give infi-nite pleafure to the lovers of that fine art, if there were any means of obtaining a copy of them, in order to acquire a more perfect knowledge of the ftate of mufic in this country under the dominion of the Arabs. The authors name is *Abbi Naffar Ben Mahommed Alpharaibi*, with the follow-ing title, as tranflated by Cafiri, the

Q king's

king's librarian, in his account of
theſe manuſcripts :

Nº. CMVI.

Abbi Naſſar Ben Mahommed Alpharaibi,
MUSICES ELEMENTA;
Adjeƈtis notis muſicis et inſtrumentorum figuris
plus triginta, &c.

After a long converſation in this
library with an ingenious friend,
who is a paſſionate admirer of Cervantes, we were going away highly
pleaſed, when the librarian who attended us with much courtefy and
good manners, recalled our attention
to a ſmall cheſt of antient coins,
which he acknowledged to have no
extraordinary merit; but they had a
very ſingular one in my eyes, as I
diſcovered them to have belonged to
the great archbiſhop of Tarragona,

Don

Don Antonio Aguftin, (whofe curious library is alfo here) and to have been the original coins which ferved him to draw up thofe learned dialogues on medals, fo univerfally admired in all countries, and which have been tranf-lated into italian and latin.—I was pleafed to fee there, a coin of the ifland of Rhodes, with the head of the famous Coloffus, and the name of the city ftamped on it, PoΔION, which the archbifhop tells us, in dialogue the fecond, they fhewed him at Rome in the church of *Santa Croce di Gierufa-lemme,* as one of the thirty pieces of money with which Judas betrayed our Saviour; but this had little effect on the learned prelate, who ftates the improbability thereof, and that Judas was more likely to have been paid

Q 2

with

with *Sicles*, or other coin of the country, as he was rewarded out of the money belonging to the public treasury. The obfervation that follows I fhall give you in the archbifhop's own words: " B. Why then do they hold this coin as a relic in Rome? A. For the fame reafon they have at the convent of Poblet *(in Catalonia)* for fhewing a large dice four times as large as the common ones, and of a jafper colour, which they fay is one of thofe, with which the foldiers played for the garments of our Lord; all thefe kind of things are very uncertain, and do not deferve fo good a name as relics, fince they were ufed as inftruments of fin."--But I am again falling into digreffions;

indulge

indulge me with one reflection more before I quit this defultory letter; and that is, that after reviewing fuch a variety of commentators which the Spanifh language affords, I lament that the great Cervantes is no longer underflood by his countrymen, and that this claffic writer, fo well acquainted with the inmoft receffes of the human heart, and who abounds with the moft beautiful allegories, yet remains without a fingle commentator!—Let me exhort you then to continue your attention to this great author, in whom nature herfelf fpeaks her own language, and I hope when I have the pleafure of feeing you again, I may without being a minifter of ftate, or yourfelf a fuitor for

Q 3

court

court favour, make you the same compliment which the earl of Oxford did to Rowe the poet, and give you joy that you can read Don Quixote in the original.

LETTER

LETTER XIV.

Revolutions and progress of the Spanish Drama.

MADRID, August 6th, 1778.

IN the present critical moment, it is impossible for an Englishman to be lukewarm, who has a true love for his country.—Though our enemies were ever so numerous, we surely are equal to dangers, let them be ever so great.---A thousand duties call me home, I long to be with you, and to take a more active part in this noble struggle; you have my best wishes, that such vigorous exertions may be crowned with success; I cannot submit to the idea of yielding even the length of a wave on our natural element:

Q 4

element: Oh faireſt iſland! may thy dominion ever be acknowledged, and thy ſpirit of freedom, commerce and happineſs, be revered and admired till time ſhall be no more! ----In this penſive ſtrain I faunter through the ſtreets of Madrid, take my evening's walk in the *Prado*, and then return home, and prepare matters for my departure from hence: but I have hitherto ſaid nothing to you of the theatre, and you will of courſe expect ſomething on that ſubject. If you will give me leave, I will take up the ſubject from a very early date, ſince I have ſeen the ſtately remains of an ancient Roman theatre at Morviedro, near Valencia, which ſhews that theſe entertainments were known in Spain under the Romans,

mans, though we cannot afcertain at what period. If you believe the report of Philoſtratus, in his life of Apollonius Tyanæus, the inhabitants of Bœtica had never feen any theatrical entertainments, and when a few indigent ſtrollers firſt appeared amongſt them, they gazed with the utmoſt aſtoniſhment at their awkward geſtures; the citizens of *Ipula* in particular were fo aſtoniſhed at a tragedy performed by thefe actors, that the audience ſtood aghaſt, and conſidered them as fo many fiends, from whom they fled with the utmoſt precipitancy; all which is fuppofed to have happened under the reign of Nero. Be this as it may, moſt probably they totally ceafed under the ravaging hand of the goth: at laſt
the

the Trobadours revived the Roman fpirit, which extended itfelf to the kingdom of Aragon, with the dramatic mufe in the days of the marquis of Villena, and at its union to Caftile, began to dawn in this latter kingdom.

The *Cancionero* of the poet Juan de la Encina, contains many dramatic pieces of his, acted during Chriftmas, Shrovetide, and Eafter, in the houfe of the Duke of Alva. Thefe entertainments not only confifted of paftoral dialogues, and fubjects of love, but were moreover adapted to the facred page, and reprefented the paffion of our faviour and other parts of fcripture, but fuch pieces could give but a feeble idea of the powers of the drama; as to their

other

other performances, the actors were moftly diffolute men, incapable, from the depravity of their manners to feel the delicate fentiments of the Greek or Roman mufe, or thofe noble paffions which inflame a generous mind; much lefs to reprefent their effects: fo that the compofitions of the times were fuitable to the turn of the actors, and reftricted to fcenes of low life, fimilar to thofe manners which conftituted their principal characters. Thefe gave origin to that noted one of the *Celeftina*, in the tragi-comedy of *Calixto* and *Melibea*, tranflated long fince into Englifh, under the title of *The Spanifh rogue*, a piece totally unworthy of the ftage, in which vice is depicted in fuch lively colours and immorality fo openly exhibited, as

to

to excite our utmost indignation. Its author is unknown, though from its classic language some have attributed it to Juan de Mena, others to Roderic de Cota. The original piece had only one act, and was afterwards compleated by Fernando de Rocas. It was first written in prose, then turned into verse by Juan de Sedeno at Salamanca, in 1540. It has been twice translated into French, first by an anonymous hand at Lyons in 1529, and reprinted at Paris in 1542, where it was again translated by Thomas Laverdin in 1598. The same dissolute temper infected the Portugueze drama ; the comedies of George Ferreira Vasconcellos, after they were printed at Evora in 1566, were immediately suppressed ; in other re-

spects

fpects he united the comic powers of Plautus and Terence; they were tranf-lated into Spanifh at Madrid in 1631, by Don Fernando Balleftros y Saave-dro, and have been again reprinted here in 1735, by Don Blas Naffarre, under the feigned name of Don Do-mingo Ferruno Quexillofo.—While the Spanifh drama laboured under all thefe difadvantages, a new Ro-fcius arofe in the perfon of Lope de Rueda of Seville, whofe pieces do honour to his memory, as well as his theatrical abilities as a performer; he was a gold-beater by trade, and it is praife fufficient for him that Cer-vantes, who was his contemporary, has fpoken highly in his favour, ad-ding that none had equalled him as an actor, or in the natural turn of

his

his dialogue and juſtneſs of character. His prologues and interludes are diſtinguiſhed by the name of *paſſos*, which ſhews the antiquity of thoſe compoſitions known at preſent by the names of *Loas*, *Entremeſes* and *Saenetes*.—Alonſo de la Vega ſucceeded Rueda as a writer and a performer, but is much inferior to him as a writer. His *Tholomea* conſiſts of eight ſcenes, but his *Duqueſa de la Roſa* is not divided into ſcenes or acts, and forms one continued ſeries.

The ſtage in thoſe days made a very mean and inconſiderable figure; Cervantes informs us, that in the time of Lope de Rueda all the apparatus of a theatre might be wrapped up in a bag, being nothing more

than

than four gilt leather ſkins, as many falſe beards and heads of hair, with three or four ſtaves. Comedies were then nothing more than paſtoral dialogues between ſhepherds and ſhepherdeſſes, with interludes, in which the ribaldry of a negro, the boaſts of a coward, and the blunders of a Biſcayner, like the bulls of our *Teague*, form the principal part, and we owe to them our *Bobadil*, a name neverthelefs of great renown in Spain, as *Falſtaff* certainly was in England, till it fell under the diſpleaſure of Shakeſpeare. Lope de Rueda was admirable in all theſe characters, and doubtleſs would have made an excellent *Abel Drugger*, though inferior in other reſpects to the great Roſcius with us. In thoſe days there were no changes of ſcenes, no

battles

battles with horfe and foot between chriftians and moors, no paffages for the actors in the centre of the ftage, the whole of which confifted of a few boards laid over benches, no machinery of any kind, an old curtain drawn acrofs, divided the part where the actors were to drefs, and where the muficians fung without the affiftance of inftruments.—Lope de Rueda died at Cordova, and in confideration of his great merit was interred in the cathedral between the two choirs near the famous jefter Luis Lopez. As an actor he had a fucceffor in Naharro of Toledo, who imitated Rueda in the low comic. The bag was replaced by trunks to hold the additional furniture, he placed the muficians before the ftage, abolifhed the

general

general ufe of falfe beards, referving them for their true characters; he introduced battles, clouds, thunder, lightning, ftorms, and fhipwreck. As a writer, Rueda was followed by Chriftoval de Caftillejo, and were it not for want of decency, his pieces would be excellent, particularly the *Conftanza*, which is in manufcript in the Efcurial. After this a more polite genius, Juan de la Cueva, of Seville, improved the Spanifh ftage, and greatly refined the language of the drama, by his foft and melodious numbers. His theatrical pieces were acted at Seville in 1579, and printed there in 1588.-----I come now to fpeak of the great author of Don Quixote as a play-writer.——The

R

title

titles of his plays are *La Gran Turquef-ca, La Batalla Naval, La Jerufalem, La Amaranta o Mayo, El Bofque Amorofo, La Arfinda*, and *La Confufa*, printed at Madrid in 1615, and reprinted in 1740. He was the firſt who divided the drama into three *Jornadas*, or acts, and was a ſtrenuous aſſertor of the true taſte of the ancients; on which account he attacked Lope de Vega with all his might, but the popular applauſe was too great in favour of his antagoniſt, who ingratiated himſelf fo much with the people by indulging their verfatile humour, added to his exuberance of fancy, and the juſtneſs of his characters, that he carried all before him, like an impetuous torrent breaking down all the barriers of oppoſition:

by

by which means, as another Shake-
fpear, Lope de Vega acquired univerfal admiration. The fecundity
of his genius was fo great, and his
productions fo rapid, that he did not
give leifure to the public to diftin-
guifh the efforts of genius from the
wild fallies of intemperate fancy;
nor could the feveral attacks of Cervantes, Villegas, Chriftoval de Mefa,
and others, prevail againft this favourite bard.----His fucceffors copied his
defects without poffeffing his beauties; Calderon, who came after him,
gave the finifhing hand to the fatal
plan of Lope, and with the fame advantages of language and wit, per-
verted the minds of the people. His
fcenes are repeated triumphs of vice,
in which the fair fex are taught to

R 2

facrifice

facrifice every thing to the impreffi-
ons of love, to defpife the advice of
tender parents, and yield to the infi-
dious arts of feducers. He gives every encouragement to licentioufnefs
and revel, and his wit was the more
dangerous from being delivered with
the moft beautiful expreffion ; his plots
are well laid and ingenioufly fupported, all which in fuch able hands
might have been applied to the moft
laudable purpofes ; though fome of
his plays have been more correct and
efcaped the general cenfure. Solis
is not inferior to Calderon in elegance and ftyle, particularly in *La
Gitanilla de Madrid*, *El Alcazar del Se-
creto*, and *Un Bobo haze ciento*. Some
of Moreto's comedies are not without
merit, fuch as *El defden con el defden*,

to

to which may be added, *El Hechizado por fuerza*, written by Zamora, alfo his *Cafligo de la miferia,* and fome others, that do honour to his memory.

With refpeɛt to tragedy, they date it from the end of the 15th century, or beginning of the 16th, when Vafco Diaz Tanco de Fregenal produced three tragedies that never were printed, wherein they may difpute the palm with the italians, who have none of an earlier date than the *Sophinifba* of Treffino, and another on the fame fubjeɛt in 1502, by Galeoto, marquifs of Carreto. To thefe may be added, the tragedies of Hernan Perez de Oliva, printed in 1586, *La Vengenza de Agamemnon* and *La Hecuba Trifle,* compofed on the model of the

R 3

greeks,

greeks. The two tragedies of *Nise Lastimosa* and *Nise Laureada*, by Bermudez, published in 1577, have not only great variety of versification and harmony of numbers, but infinite merit in their compositions ; the same may be said of the tragedies of Juan de la Cueva ; as for those of Gabriel Lasso, they fall much short of the former, either in language or -invention. Cervantes praises those of *La Isabela*, *La Filis* and *La Alexandra*, which were written by Lupercio de Argensola.

In 1609 five tragedies of Christoval de Virues were printed, which had but a middling reputation, no more than that of the '*Pompeyo* of Christoval de Mesa in 1618: as to

Lope

Lope de Vega, I referve myfelf to fpeak to you more fully concerning him in my next letter.------Little can be faid in favour of the tragedy of *Dona Ines de Caftro*, by Mexia de la Cerda, or *Los Siete Infantes de Lara*, by Zarate, in 1651, which, with fome other pieces void of particular merit, brings us near to the demife of Charles the 2d.

Since the acceffion of the Houfe of Bourbon, the tragic mufe has been chafter, and the genius of the French drama has rendered them more correct. Don Auguftin de Montiano, in his tragedies of *Virginia*, and *Ataulpho*, publifhed in 1750 and 1753, may be ftiled the Spanifh Sophocles, and be faid to be equal to

 Corneille

Corneille and Racine in the juftnefs of the drama, uniting the fire of the Gallic eagle with the melody of the fwan. Mr. Hermilly has tranflated his *Virginia* into French, as well as his firft difcourfe upon Spanifh tragedy which precedes it, and to him I muft refer you for the prefent.

Adieu !

LOPE DE VEGA.

LETTER XV.

Sketch of the life and character of the famous poet Lope de Vega.

MADRID, Auguſt 15th, 1778.

THOUGH I perfectly agree with you in opinion relating to our immortal Shakeſpeare, yet I cannot refrain from doing that juſtice to his contemporary Lope de Vega which his moſt extraordinary talents deſerve ; I ſhall therefore attempt to give you the character of this great poet, which is no eaſy taſk when his amazing abilities are conſidered; however, I ſhall venture to proceed as this will be the laſt letter I ſhall write to you from hence.

Lope

Lope Felix de Vega Carpio, born the 25th November 1562, was the fon of Felix Vega de Carpio, a gentleman of Madrid, who had the reputation of being a very good poet, a turn which he obferved with rapture in his child from its infancy, and which the fond parent cherifhed with the greateft delight. At five years of age young Lope could read fpanifh and latin fluently, and even make verfes which he exchanged with his fchool-fellows for pictures and other trifles. His father, charmed with this furprizing dawn of genius, fpared no pains to cultivate a darling plant that feemed to encourage the moft flattering expectations. At the age of twelve, Lope was mafter of the latin tongue and the art of rhetoric; could

dance

dance and fence with eafe and dexterity, and fing with a tolerable tafte.
---Endowed with thefe accomplifh-
ments, he became an orphan at his
firft entrance into the world with every preffure of diftrefs, and was taken
into the fervice of the bifhop of Avila, in whofe praife he wrote feveral
paftorals, and made his firft dramatic effay, with a comedy intitled *La
Paftoral de Jacinto.* He foon after
quitted his patron, went to the
univerfity of Alcala, where he ftudi-
ed philofophy, and took a degree,
then returned to Madrid and became
crétary to the Duke of Alva, who
entrufted him with his moft weighty
concerns. Encouraged by his new
Mecenas, he again tuned his lyre,
and fung his praife in a poem intitled

tled *Arcadia*. About this time he married Dona Ifabela de Urbina, a lady of
fafhion, on account of whofe gallantries
he foon after fought a duel, and having grievoufly wounded his antago-
nift, fled to Valencia, where he lived
fome years; after which he returned
again to Madrid, where lofing his
wife, he felt himfelf animated with
a military ardour, and repaired to
Cadiz to embark on board the great
armada, fitting out by Philip the 2d,
againft Queen Elizabeth. In this
fleet he failed for Lifbon in company with his brother, a lieutenant
in the fpanifh navy, who loft his
life in that expedition. Our poet
had his fhare of the misfortunes of
that difappointed fleet, and appeared
at Madrid without a fingle friend,

became

became fecretary to the marquifs of Malpica, and afterwards to the count of Lemos. Though his firft marriage was fo unfuccefsful, he was in hopes of being more fortunate in that ftate with Dona Juana de Guardia, a lady of rank whom he foon after loft. Inconfolable at thefe repeated afflictions, he entered into the ecclefiaftic ftate, was ordained a prieft and appointed head chaplain to a congregation of priefts at Madrid, though he ftill courted the mufes, making this the chief relaxation that foftened his forrows. He was now in the zenith of his poetic glory, and his reputation became fo univerfal, that pope Urban the eighth fent him the degree of doctor in divinity, and the crofs of the order of

Malta,

Malta, added to a lucrative poft in
the apoftolic exchequer, which Lope
held to his death, which happened
in his feventy-third year, to the great
regret of the court, and every learned
man in the kingdom. The duke of
Sefa, who was his patron and executor,
caufed him to be interred at his own
expence with fuch pomp and magnificence as had never been feen before for a private perfon; the duke
invited all the grandees of the kingdom, who attended in perfon, in
token of their concern at the lofs of
fo diftinguifhed a character. The
funeral obfequies lafted three days,
all the clergy of the king's chapel
affifted, three bifhops officiated pon-
tifically, and three of the moft eloquent orators exerted themfelves in
praife

praise of the deceased, adding new laurels to the fame of Lope de Vega, with whom, when living, many princes gloried in being acquainted. Pope Urban wrote him a letter in answer to a dedication of his poem in favour of Mary queen of Scots, intitled *Corona tragica de Maria Stuardo.* Cardinal Barbarini held a very intimate correspondence with him, as did many other cardinals and noblemen, who courted his friendship. When he walked in the streets, he was gazed upon and followed as a prodigy, he was, moreover, loaded with presents, and by the rapid sale of his numerous works soon amassed a considerable fortune, and acquired a capital of 150.000 ducats, besides his annual income of fifteen

hundred

hundred ducats, arising out of his benefices and employments; so great was the fertility of his genius, the amasing readiness of his wit and rapidity of thought, added to his animated expression, that perhaps there never was a poet in the world, either antient or modern, that could be compared to him.—His lyric compositions and fugitive pieces, with his prose essays, form a collection of fifty volumes, besides his dramatic works, which make twenty-six volumes more; exclusive of four hundred scriptural dramatic pieces, called in Spain *Autos Sacramentales*, all which were successively brought on the stage; and what is still more extraordinary, speaking of his printed works, in one of his pastorals to

Claudio

Claudio he fays they form the leaft part of what ftill remained in his clofet. It appears from his own authority, that he ufed conftantly to write five fheets a day, which multiplied by the days of his life, would make 133,225 fheets; then reckoning the number of verfes correfponding to each fheet, it will appear that exclufive of profe he wrote 21,316,000 verfes, an unheard of exertion and facility of verfification ! Our author poffeffing an inexhauftible fund, which like the fire of Vefuvius, continually afforded new matter, and blazed out inceffantly. So extraordinary was the rapidity of his genius, he would often finifh a play in twenty-four hours, and fome comedies in lefs than five hours, with as much correctnefs and

S   elegance

elegance in his verfe, as the moft laboured pieces of other writers of his
time. Such was the contemporary
of Sir Philip Sidney, Shakefpeare,
and Spencer ; in his *Laurel de Apollo*
he has celebrated all the good poets
of his time, but none were more univerfally praifed from all parts than
himfelf ; his furprifing faculties were
fuch, that in his dramatic pieces he
broke through all rules of art, yet
fuch was his fuccefs, that he was
conflantly the favourite of the public, and drew perpetual burfts of
applaufe.--- It was not his fault if
his fucceffors had not his talents to
conceal their defects, and only imitated his imperfections, rendering the
Spanifh drama infupportable when

deprived

deprived of the beauties of Lope: this was foreseen by Cervantes, who reproaches our poet with destroying the rules of the drama, as laid down by the ancients, in order to court popular applause; to obtain which he lost sight of every idea of nature, or good taste, adding, that the probability of fable dwindled in his hands, and was wasted away by the enchanting magic of verse; all unity of time and place was annihilated; his heroes came out of their cradles, and wandered from east or west as lovers or combatants, put on the cowl of monks, died in cloysters, and worked miracles on the stage. The scene is transported from Italy to Flanders, and as easily shifted from Valencia to Mexico. Footmen discourse like

 courtiers,

courtiers, princes like bullies, and ladies like chambermaids. The actors appear in legions, often feventy at a time, and clofe with numerous proceffions, which is ftill kept up with us, as well as opening graves, and burying the dead, performing the moft awful rites of mortality by way of amufement, which for my part I muft own makes my heart recoil at the difmal fight ; nor can the moft captivating language of Shakefpeare overcome my feelings at this glaring indecorum.

So fenfible was Lope of the wildnefs of his imagination, and how wantonly he fported with the confidence of the public, that fpeaking of himfelf,

himself, he acknowledges his fault in
the following words ;

> Mas ninguno de todos llamar puedo
> Mas barbaro que yo, pues contra el arte
> Me atrevo a dar preceptos, y me dexo
> Llevar de la vulgar corriente, a donde
> Me llaman ignorante, Italia y Francia.

And again,

> Y escrivo por el arte, que inventaron
> Los que el vulgar aplauso pretendieron
> Porque como los paga el vulgo, es Justo
> Hablarle en necio, para darle gusto.

That is, " that he was sensible of the
reproaches Italy and France would
make him for breaking through all
rules to please the ignorant public,
but since it was they, that paid for it,
they had a right to be pleased in
their own way."

I have

I have now given you both fides of the queſtion, refpecting this great man ; were I to fpeak to you of his perfonal virtues, they are yet fuperior to his literary talents.   His benevolence and charity towards the indigent and diſtreſſed was fo great, that he always extended his hand to the needy, infomuch that notwithſtanding his confiderable fortune and income, not more than fix thoufand ducats were found at his death.—O illuſtrious bard, if an Englifhman is not capable of doing juſtice to thy poetical numbers, and the harmony of thy verfe, accept at leaſt of this tribute to the goodnefs of thy heart.

LETTER XVI.

City of Burgos. Tomb of the Cid, and of king John the Second.

BURGOS, 15th Auguſt, 1778.

THE next day after I had the pleaſure of addreſſing my laſt letter to you, I ſet out from the town of Madrid, and paſſing through Segovia and Valladolid, arrived at the antient city of Burgos, where I propoſe making a halt for a few days, to enjoy a little reſt after a fatiguing journey, and to look about me in this venerable city, dwindled from its former ſplendour, but ſtill the reſidence of many noble families, il-

S 4

luſtrious

luftrious for their lineage and military atchievements.—In this city Edward, of England, eldeſt ſon of our
king Henry the 3d, was knighted in
1254, by king Alfonſo the wiſe, and
married the princeſs Eleanor of Caſtile, that amiable woman, who when
her huſband was wounded with a poiſoned arrow in Paleſtine, ſucked the
venom out of the wound, and reſtored him to health. Nor was the
Engliſh nation wanting in acknow-
ledgments to this affectionate princeſs, who dying of a fever on her
journey to Scotland, was conveyed
to Weſtminſter with great funeral
pomp, and elegant ſtone croſſes were
erected at each place where the corpſe
reſted.—The cathedral of Burgos is a
moſt magnificent ſtructure in the gothic

thic tafle, and has a great refem-
blance to York minfler.——As this is the
country of that famous Spanifh hero
Roderic Diaz de Bivar, commonly called the *Cid*, who lived in the days of
Ferdinand the ıfl, I did not forget
to vifit his fhrine at the church
of *San Pedro de Cardena*, about fix
miles from hence, belonging to the
benedictine monks ; I went there
with the fame curiofity as I fhould to
view the tomb of Guy earl of War-
wick, or any of our renowned Englifh champions.--I accordingly mounted my courfer with becoming gravity, and repaired to his tomb, which
is in a particular chapel of the church
of San Pedro, with the arms of all
his relations depicled on the walls,
and a long fcroll of his genealogy and
exploits.

exploits. In the veſtry they have an original portrait of him, done immediately after his death.——His memory is held in ſuch veneration, that the good man, who ſhewed me every thing, twice called him a ſaint, but ſtopped ſhort and correcled himſelf. No warrior, however, has had ſo much ſaid of him; he has a ſeparate chronicle of his life and aclions, in one volume in folio, printed in 1552 by command of the infant Don Ferdinand afterwards emperor, who gave this commiſſion to Velerado abbot of the convent of San Pedro. The writer ſays he extracled it from the original chronicle in the archives of that houſe; but in that he is miſtaken, for it was not an original but an antient copy according to the teſtimony

of

of Berganza, a monk of the same house, who about twenty years ago, published its antiquites, in two volumes in folio, and suppofes that the original chronicle of the Cid was firft written in arabic, by a converted moor, with his fon, who were fervants to the Cid, and was afterwards tranflated into Spanifh. The archbifhop of Toledo, and Don Lucas de Tuy, are fpoken of in this chronicle, tho' they flourifhed in the middle of the 13th century, and the Cid died in 1099, therefore this chronicle muft have been continued by another hand as father Sarmiento obferves, but without impeaching the veracity of its contents. The general chronicle of Spain was compiled by order of Alfonfo the wife, yet who-

ever

ever reads what is said of the Cid, and *vice versa*, will doubt whether the general chronicle was copied from that of the Cid, or the latter from the former: but they still have their share of merit as far as they elucidate the manners and cuſtoms of the times, when diveſted of the fables and ſuperſtition with which they are clouded. Since the burning of Don Quixote's library, not only romances but many of the chronicles are become very ſcarce, and they are now reprinting a general collection of them at Madrid.— In vain have I ſearched for *Artus de Bretana*, who was turned into a crow, ſince which time no Engliſhman, according to Cervantes, will ever kill a crow. The elucidation

tion of this point I muſt leave to yourſelf.

To return to the Cid, every thing belonging to this great warrior is ſacred; his ſwords are admired and ſhewn as great curioſities; one of them is in the king's armoury at Madrid, and is called *Colada*, in alluſion to its fine temper; on one ſide it has theſe four letters S I S I. and on the other NO NO. According to Garibay the hiſtorian, the Cid took this ſword from the Count of Barcelona, when in arms againſt the king of Aragon.--The other ſword was called the *Tizona*, " The flaming ſword," which he wreſted from Bucar lord of Tunis. This ſword belonged afterwards to the Infant Don Ramiro of

Navarre,

Navarre, from whofe houfe it was given to the family of Peralta. Sandoval, bifhop of Pamplona, in his chronicle defcribes this fword which he faw, and fays, on one fide it had thefe words *Yo foy la Tifona que fue hecha en la era de mil y quarenta.* On the other fide *Ave Maria gratiæ plena. Dominus.*—The Cid was defcended from Lain Calvo, one of the judges of Caftile : he left two daughters, Dona Sola, married to the Infant Don Pedro eldeft fon of Peter king of Aragon, and Dona Elvina to Don Ramon Sancho, eldeft fon of Sancho Garcias king of Navarre. His panegyrifts have entered into endlefs details in his praife; even his horfe *Babieca* has not been omitted, and is faid to have lived forty-four years. Having taken

a folemn

a folemn farewell of this manfion, which was built on the remains of a palace belonging to this hero, I returned back to Burgos, ftriking off a little to the right, to vifit *Miraflores* a convent of Carthufians, given to that order by John the 2d king of Caftile, who is interred in their church before the great altar, and has a beautiful marble monument adorned with infinite workmanfhip. This tomb the people call here a *pantheon.*—I faw in the choir, an original portrait of his daughter Ifabella queen of Caftile, who appears to have been very handfome. There is a full length picture of her in the palace of Buen Retiro at Madrid.—You will fay that I have quitted my ground fince I have penetrated into old Caftile,

tile, and have deferted the poets for the chronicles, but allow me this digreffion in favour of a hero who infpired the great Corneille, and furnifhed a fubject for the fublime genius of that celebrated poet.---What would the bold Cid fay, if he was to appear again on the horizon ? If he, who to preferve his precedency broke the chair of the French ambaffador in the prefence of the pope, was to fee his own countrymen making peace with the moors, and foliciting leave of the pope to eat fifh in lent.   Not like the devout heroes of thofe and fubfequent times, when the Englifh and French, according to Rapin, fought a bloody battle juft before lent, to intercept a convoy of fifh, and num-

bers

bers loſt their lives to aſcertain who ſhould dine on a herring.

☞ In the reign of Henry VI. when John Duke of Bedford was regent of France in 1429, he ſent from Paris to the Engliſh army then beſieging Orleans, a convoy of ſalt fiſh, the lent ſeaſon being come, which with the artillery and ammunition, made near five hundred carts, under the command of ſir John Faſtolf, one of the braveſt generals in the Engliſh army. The convoy was attacked on the road to Orleans, by the French under the count of Clermont, at the head of three thouſand men, but they were repulſed with great ſlaughter by the Engliſh, loſing ſix ſcore lords and about ſix hundred men. This action was called " The battle of Herrings."

LETTER

LETTER XVII.

Privileges of the different orders of nobility in Spain.

BURGOS, 4th SEPT. 1778.

YOU afk me what fort of figure the country gentlemen make in Spain, and who are the people ftiled *Hidalgos.* To the firft I fhall anfwer that as the *Cortes,* or parliaments have been abolifhed ever fince the acceffion of the houfe of Bourbon, all the confequence of the country gentlemen has ceafed. The *Hidalgos* claim a defcent from thofe valiant foldiers who retired into Caftile, and the mountains of Afturias, and other re-

mote

mote parts of Spain, on the invasion
of the moors, where having fortified
themselves, they succeffively defcended into the plains, in proportion to
the fuccefs of their arms : ----from
the notoriety of their perfons, or the
lands they became poffeffed of, they
acquired the appellation of *Hidalgos
notorios, Hidalgos de folar conocido,* or
de cafa folariega; of thefe according to
Hernando Mexia, there are three
forts, the 1ft being lords of places,
villages, towns, or caftles, from
whence they took their firnames, as
the Guzmans, Mendozas, Laras, Gui-
varas, and others; the 2nd, who recovered any fortrefs from the moors,
as the *Ponces* of *Leon*, and others; and
the third fort, from the places where
they refided or held jurifdiction, as

T 2

Rodrigo

Rodrigo de Narvaez was called of Antequera, from being *Alcayde* there. But this definition is not confidered as exact or conclufive by Otalora, another civilian, who fays that the true meaning of *Hidalgos de folar conocido* is explained by the laws of Caftile, to be a well known manfion or poffeffion, the nature of which is particularly explained in the laws of the *partidas*, lib. 5. tit. 35. which defcribe three forts of tenures called *Devifa, Solariega* and *Behetria*. By the firft, lands are devifed by the anceftor, *folar* is a tenure upon another perfon's manor, and obliges the owner to receive the lord of the fee when neceffity obliges him to travel, and *Behetria* is in the nature of an *allodium*.

In

In proportion as thefe Aborigines gained ground on the Moors, and increafed in their numbers, many private perfons diftinguifhed themfelves by their valour, and obtained teftimonies of their fervices, called *carlas de merced*, which ferved them as a foundation of their birth and good defcent, without which documents their pofterity could not make it appear; and if from a lapfe of time, or other unavoidable accidents, fuch proof fhould happen to be loft, or deftroyed, the law affords them a remedy under thefe circumftances, by a declaration importing, that fuch perfons as are fuppofed to have had fuch certificates, may be relieved by making it appear, that their anceftors, time immemorial, have always

T 3

been

been held and reputed as *Hidalgos*, and enjoyed the privileges of such, from a strong presumption in their favour; the possession of land having equal force to any other document, which is fully set forth in the *prag-matica* of Cordova. To these executory letters are granted, *cartas ex-ecutorias*, expressive of their privileges, and for the better regulation of these matters, proper officers are appointed in the chancery courts, called *alcaldes de los hidalgos*, who ought to be *hidalgos* themselves, and hold jurisdiction in these cases, and no others; but even here innovations have taken place, for as these grants flow from the sovereign, who is the fountain of honour, some are declared *Hidalgos de sangre*, by right of de-

scent,

fcent, and others *de privilegio*, or by office, in which, the will of the fovereign has made amends for any deficiency of blood.

There is a fet of people near Segovia at a place called Zamarramala, who are exempt from tribute on account of the care they take in fending proper perfons every night to the caftle of Segovia to keep centinel----one cries out *Vela, vela, hao*, and the other blows a horn, from whence they have been titled *hidalgos by the horn*. In Catalonia thofe gentlemen who are ftiled *Hombresde Pareja*, are confidered the fame as *hidalgos* in Caftile, and were fo called from the word *parejar*, to equip, this name being given as a diftinction by Bo-

T 4

rela

relo the 4th, count of Barcelona, at the fiege of that city in 965, who fummoning all his vaffals to come to his affiftance againft the moors, nine hundred horfemen well mounted and equipped joined him, and with their aid he took the city, and this appellation has been given in honourable remembrance of this loyal action.

- You will of courfe be defirous to know what are the privileges that thefe noble Hidalgos enjoy ? The principal of them are as follows :

1. The firft and greateft privilege which they hold by law is to enjoy all pofts of dignity and honour in the church and ftate, with liberty when churchmen of having a plurality of benefices.

benefices. They are qualified for receiving all orders of knighthood, and are to be preferred in all embassies, governments, and public commissions.

2. When they are examined as witnesses in civil and criminal cases, their depositions are to be taken in their own houses, without being obliged to quit them to go to those of others.

3. In all churches, processions and other public acts or assemblies, they are to have the next place of honour and precedency after the officers of justice, conforming themselves to particular customs.

4. They

4. They are not obliged to accept of any challenge for combat, suppofing fuch were allowed of, but from thofe who are their equals.

5. Though it is forbid to guardians to purchafe the eftates of minors, this does not extend to *Hidalgos* in whom the law does not fuppofe any fraud, and they may purchafe them publicly.

6. They are permitted to be feated in courts of juftice in prefence of the judges, from the refpect and honour due to them. They have alfo feats in the courts of chancery, in confideration of their birth, which gives them a right to be near the perfons of princes.

7. Their

7. Their perfons are free from arreft for debt, nor can any attachment
be laid on their dwelling houfes, furniture, apparel, arms, horfes, or
mules, in immediate ufe, nor can
they make a ceffion of their eftates,
nor be diftreffed in fuits of law, further than their circumftances will admit of, but are to be allowed a rea-
fonable and decent maintenance for
their fupport.

8. In cafes of imprifonment for
criminal matters, they are to be
treated differently from others. They
are generally confined to their own
houfes with a fafe guard, or under
arreft upon their honour, or allowed
the city or town they live in, and in
particular cafes are fent into caftles.

9. When

9. When punishments are inflicted for criminal cases, they are to be less severe to them than to others, as they are not to suffer ignominious punishments, such as public shame, whipping, gallies, nor are they to be hanged, but beheaded, except in cases of treason or heresy.----In cases that do not imply a corporal punishment but a pecuniary one, they are treated with more rigour, and pay a larger fine than others.

10. They are not to be put to the rack or torture, except for such heinous crimes as are particularly specified by the laws.

11. When there are title deeds or other writings or papers in which two

or

or more perfons have an equal right or property, and require a particular charge, they are to be given up by preference to the cuftody of an *Hidalgo*, if any of the parties are fuch.

12. The daughter of an Hidalgo enjoys every privilege of her birth, though married to a commoner, and a woman who is not an *Hidalga*, enjoys all thefe privileges when fhe is a widow, following the fortune of her hufband.----But if the widow is an *Hidalga*, and the late hufband was a commoner, fhe falls into the ftate of her hufband after his death, though fhe had the privileges of her birth during his life.

13, They are free from all duties, called *Pechos, Pedidos, Monedas, Marteniegas*

niegas Contribuciones, as well royal as civil, and all other levies of whatever kind they may be, with a reserve for fuch as are for the public benefit, in which they are equally concerned, fuch as the repairing the highways, bridges, fountains, walls, deſtruction of locuſts, and other vermin.

14. They are free from perſonal ſervice, and from going to the wars, except when the king attends in perſon; even then they are not to be forced, but invited, and acquainted that the royal ſtandard is diſplayed.

15. No perſons whatever can be quartered upon, or lodged in, their houſes, except when the king, queen, prince or infantes are on the road,

road, as in such cafes even the houfes of the clergy are not exempt.

16. They cannot be compelled to accept of the office of receiver of the king's rents, or any other employment which is confidered as mean and derogatory to their dignity and rank.

17. By a particular cuftom confirmed by royal authority in that part of Caftile beyond the Ebro, baftards fucceed to their parents, and enjoy their honours contrary to the royal and common law.

18. If a lady who marries a commoner fhould be a queen, dutchefs, marchionefs, or countefs, for they

have

have no barons in Caftile, not only does not lofe her rank, but conveys her titles to her hufband, who holds them in right of his wife.

Thefe are the general privileges which the *Hidalgos* enjoy; there are fome others of lefs confequence, as well as particular grants to certain perfons and families. An antient and ridiculous cuftom is faid to be obferved by noble ladies' who are widows of plebeians, in order to recover their birthright, for which purpofe they carry a packfaddle on their fhoulders to their hufband's grave, then throwing it down and ftriking it three times, fay, " villain, take thy villainy, for I will abide by my nobility," and then they recover their privileges again.

As

As for the titles of marquifs and count, which are called *Titles of Ca-stile*, they feem to be merely honorary, and give much the fame rank as our baronets do in England. The merchants of Cadiz feem fond of them, and when they grow rich, they are eafily obtained.

The grandees of Spain form the true nobility of the country, and were originally divided into three claffes, the firft had the privilege of fpeaking covered in the *cortes* in prefence of the king, the fecond were covered after they had fpoken, and the third were only *ad honores*, with the title of excellency, and the privilege of appearing with the others in public affemblies ; fince the extinction of the

U

cortes,

cortes, their privileges have dwindled. When the death of the marquifs de Valdermofo was mentioned in the Madrid gazette, of the 6th of April, 1773, as a Grandee of the fecond clafs, it was contradicted in the following one, adding that he only enjoyed the title *ad honores.*

The oldeft duke in Spain feems to be the duke of Medina Sidonia, which title was firft granted by king John the fecond the 17th of February 1445, to John Alonfo de Guzman, third count of Niebla. Our oldeft duke at prefent in England, is defcended from Charles Howard, created duke of Norfolk by Richard the third, on June 28th, 1483.

If

If after this you aſk me what ſort of a life the *hidalgos* lead? I muſt inform you, it is much the ſame with that of Don Diego de Miranda, in Don Quixote, who gave the following account of himſelf. " My name is Don " Diego de Miranda ; I am an *hidalgo*, " and a native of the village, where " with God's permiſſion, we ſhall dine " to day ; my fortune is more than " moderate, and I live with my wife, " children and friends ; my chief " amuſements are hunting and fiſh- " ing, yet I have neither hawks nor " greyhounds, but ſome decoy par- " tridges, and a bold ferret ; I have " about ſix dozen of books, ſome in " Spaniſh, and others in latin, a few " of hiſtory, and others of devotion ; " thoſe of knight errantry I have not

U 2

" yet

" yet fuffered to come within my
" doors.   I delight (*) more in pro-

All thefe lines in the text after this mark to the
end of the paragraph, are omitted in the new tranflation of Don Quixote, by Charles Henry Wilmot, Efq;
London, 1774, as well as thofe lines which immediately follow here:---

" Sancho, who was all attention to the account
which the *Hidalgo* gave of his life and manners, which
feemed to him to be commendable and holy, and that
fuch a good liver ought to work miracles, threw himfelf off from his afs, and with great hurry ran towards Don Diego, and laid hold of his right ftirrup,
and with a fervent heart, and tears in his eyes, kiffed
his foot many times; which being obferved by the
Hidalgo, What are you about brother? he faid,
what does this mean? permit me to proceed, faid
Sancho, for your worfhip feems to me to be the firft
faint I have ever feen on horfeback.   I am no faint,
anfwered the gentleman, but a great finner; but you,
good brother, are a worthy man, from the fimplicity of
your manners.   Sancho returned to his faddle, having at laft extorted a fmile from the truly melancholy afpect of his mafter, and caufed further admiration to Don Diego.---Don Quixote afked him how
many children he had, &c.

" fane

" fane books than in devout ones,
" provided that they are not immo-
" ral; that the language is elegant,
" and that the mind is captivated
" with the ingenuity of their inven-
" tion, though of thefe we have few
" in Spain.   I fometimes dine with
" my neighbours and friends, and of-
" ten invite them ; my repafts are
" plain and 'neat, but plenty dwells
" under my roof.   I never find fault
" with my acquaintance, nor do I con-
" fent to the murmurs of others in
" my prefence.   I don't pry into the
" life and converfation of my neigh-
" bours, nor look fharply into their
" actions.   I hear mafs every day,
" divide my eftate with the poor,
" without making boafts of my cha-
" rity, not to let hypocrify or vanity

U 3   " take

" take poffeffion of my heart, ene-
" mies that gently fteal upon the moft
" guarded minds. I endeavour to
" reconcile thofe who are at variance.
" I am devout to the Virgin Mary,
" and I place my truft in the in-
" finite mercy of God."

With refpect to their lineage, if you want further information, confult Penafiel de Contreras, a famous Spanifh antiquary, who, in compliment to Philip the 3d, drew up a genealogical tree of one hundred and eighteen defcents, from Adam down to that fovereign; and, to pleafe the then prime minifter, duke of Lerma, of the houfe of *Guzman*, he formed another pedigree of one hundred and twenty-one defcents, alfo from Adam down

down to the duke, connecting him with the sovereign, in the person of Tros, king of Troy, (great grand father of Priam and Æneas) by his two sons Assaracus and Ilus; from one of which Philip descended, and the minister from the other! What a contagious distemper is flattery, and how rapidly it flies from pole to pole. In the north, John Miffen paid a similar compliment, deduced from Adam, to his sovereign the king of Sweden; and William Slater did as much for James the 1st, king of Great-Britain.

Adieu!

LETTER XVIII.

*Lordſhip of Biſcay.—Antient poetry in the Vaſ-
cuenſe language.*

BILBAO, October 10th, 1778.

AFTER travelling over a great
many mountains, I at laſt arrived at this pleaſant town, which
cloſes my expedition through the
Spaniſh dominions. As for the antient language of this country called
the *Vaſcuenſe*, we are the more perplexed and in the dark, as all the
books extant in that language are
modern ; ſo that, it is a very difficult
matter to give any preciſe ideas or
fix any ſtandard of their tongue, and
much

much lefs of their poetry, as the natives feem to have referved a particular corner of Parnaffus to themfelves, in which they have neither rivals nor competitors.

If the poem in *Vafcuenfe* mentioned by Argote de Molina in his difcourfe on fpanifh poetry is as antient as the actions which it relates ; we fhould have a tolerable document to form a judgement of the poetry of thefe people, about the beginning of the fourteenth century, that is towards the year 1320. If we exclude this record, we have no other fpecimen of their poetry, except fome fpiritual hymns of Juan de Aramburu, and thofe of Bernardo de Gazteluzar printed at Pau in 1686, and another

nother anonymous poet mentioned by Larramendi. The moſt famous of their poets is ſaid to be Juan de Echeverri, a Doctor in Divinity, who compoſed the life of Chriſt and of ſome ſaints, in this ancient verſe, which were printed at Bayonne in 1650.—As for my part I have in vain ſtudied the language in the grammar of Laramendi, and am willing to take the people on their words, who aſſure me it is very harmonious; nor can I give you any ſatisfactory account of the antiquity of the inhabitants who are ſuppoſed to have peopled Ireland. The iriſh antiquaries agree that the colonies of Mileſians came from Brigantia to Ireland, and O'Flaherty and Keating aſſert, that Florian de Ocampo an

old

old ſpaniſh writer, proves in his chronicle, that the Brigantines of Ireland owe their origin to Spain, and
ſo paſſed into Wales; but for my
part, as I am as little verſed in the
iriſh tongue as I am in the Biſcayan,
it is not in my power to give you
any lights on this ſubjeᵭt. ----- Who
knows? if I had had the good fortune to read the poems of Oſſian
in the original, perhaps it might have
afforded ſome aſſiſtance, and I might
have recovered from obſcurity ſome
Biſcay warrior, like Fingal, who lord-
ed it over theſe mountains, and perhaps did feats which the moſt harmonious verſes have done juſtice to, that
now lie buried beyond the reach of
our moſt profound antiquaries.

The

The inhabitants of the lordſhip of Biſcay, as a free people, enjoy a great many excluſive rights and privileges, beyond the Caſtilians, or any other ſubjects of Spain. Theſe rights are ſet forth in a folio entitled, *El Fuero de los Cavalleros de Viſcaya*, Medina 1575, which book I have ſought for in vain, as well as a geographic poem deſcribing the kingdom of Galicia, in alexandrine verſe, by Luis de Molina, printed at Mondonedo, in 1550.

An iriſhman, whoſe name is William Bowles, who having been employed for theſe twenty years as an engineer in the king of Spain's ſervice, and has travelled over moſt parts of Spain, has lately publiſhed ſome very curi-

ous

ous memoirs at Madrid, dedicated to the prefent king of Spain, intended as an introduction to the natural hif- tory and phyfical geography of that kingdom; amongft other things he has given a pretty full account of the genius and manners of the Bifcayans, and has taken fome pains to draw a comparifon between them and the antient irifh; but this point ftill ad- mits of further illuftration, from the very precarious foundation of all rea- foning, arifing merely on a fuppofed fimilitude of manners and cuftoms: tho' I readily agree with him in the account he gives of their hofpitable difpofition and chearful temper, ad- ded to the utmoft induftry in culti- vating their rugged mountains, by which means they have rendered the

greateft

greateſt part of their country both pleaſant and fruitful. They, moreover, apply themſelves cloſely to foreign commerce and navigation, having been always deemed induſtrious traders, and expert and ſkilful mariners, inſomuch that for the whale fiſhery ſo far back as 1575, the Engliſh merchants were obliged to ſend to Biſcay *for men ſkilful in the catching of the whale, and ordering of the oil; and one cooper, ſkilful to ſet up the ſtaved caſk.* It further appears, that we not only loſt all memory of that trade for many centuries, which we had known in the days of king Alfred, but that the Biſcayans carried it on long before we attempted it again, as well on account of the oil as for the whalebone: the firſt Engliſh ſhip

that

that went on that trade into the bay of St. Lawrence, according to Hackluyt, in 1594, found part of the cargoe of two Bifcay fhips that had been wrecked there, three years before. But, becaufe I am drawing nearer to England, you will fay, I am again running into digreffions, and it matters not, who had that fifhery or any other maritime commerce at that time, provided we can hold it at prefent, , and make good the old maxim, *Imperator Maris, Terræ Dominus.*

LETTER XIX.

Departure from Bilbao for England by sea. Sentence of the inquisition against Don Pablo de Olavide.

BILBAO, 10th Dec. 1778.

I HAVE been detained in this country longer than I expected, waiting in hopes of a friend who was desirous of coming to England along with me; this delay, however, has enabled me to furnish you with a very extraordinary piece of news, no less than the sentence of the Inquisition, against an unfortunate gentleman, who at one time was in high favour at court, and from whose abilities the greatest expectations were formed.

You

You may perhaps have heard, some
years ago, of the projects of this government to colonise the defert
mountains of Sierra Morena, in Andalufia.   The *Cedula*, or grant for
this undertaking was iffued by the
king in 1767, and contains 79 articles.   The intention of the court was
to invite 6000 catholic germans and
flemings, who were to be fettled there
with proper encouragement, in order
to introduce agriculture and manu-
factures, as well as population in that
defolate diftrict, for the carrying on
of which the infpection and manage-
ment of the whole was given to Don
Pablo de Olavide, *affiftente*, or governor of Seville, from whofe knowledge
and patriotifm it was expected a flourifhing colony would foon arife; ac-

X

cordingly

cordingly several towns were built,
and the country soon began to wear
a new aspect, but unfortunately this
gentleman was some time ago taken
up at Madrid, hurried away from his
house, and confined in the dark prisons of the inquisition, and after a
long and painful imprisonment, was
brought in the most humiliating manner before his judges, and the following sentence, which I inclose you
herewith, pronounced against him,
on which I shall make no comments,
as your own judgement will give you
an idea of the benevolence and libe-
rality of sentiment that reigned in
that assembly; shew you the weight
of the charge, the manner by which
it is proved, and of course how far
he was deserving of the dreadful

X   punish-

punifhment that followed: by which
the prifoner, without having his loy-
alty or fidelity to his fovereign called
in queftion, becomes the moft unhappy fubject poffible and in an infinite-
ly worfe flate than the moft wretched
perfon in the kingdom. I

I now lay down my fpanifh lance,
as well as the golden helmet of Mam-
brino, and am haftening home as
faft as poffible, referving only my
Toledo blade, made by that famous
artift Andrew Ferrara.—The din of
war founds conftantly in my ears ; it
is too late at prefent to look back !
If I fall, may it be glorioufly in defence of my country, my beloved
country, whofe rights I fervently
wifh may ever remain inviolate ! let

X 2

who

who will be the invader.—— Methinks
I fee you caft a difdainful look towards the fpanifh mufe; let me then
have recourfe to your admired Petrarch, and in bidding farewell to
the continent, as I fhall embark at
this port, I clofe our correfpondence
with the following lines of that favourite poet :

 Del empia Babilonia ond' e fugitta
 Ogni vergogna, ond ogni bene e fuori,
 Albergo di dolor, madre d'errori
 Son fugit io per allungar la vita.

Narrative

Narrative of an Auto de Fe, held the 27th of November, 1778, in the cause of Paul de Olavide, before Don Joseph Escalzo, and Don Bernardo Loigorri, inquisitors of the court, with the assist-ance of several persons of rank called to attend thereat, who were not even charged with silence, out of charity, as is customary on similar occasions.

P R E S E N T,

Duque de Granada and his chaplain Mosa Xaraba
Cerda
Don Patricio Buftos
Don Rosendo Paraf-puelo
Marquifs de Casa-tremanes
Duke of Hijar
Marquifs of Belamazan

Count of Mora
Duke of Abrantes
Don Joseph Eulate
Don Ant. Monsagrati
Don Manuel Trevisano
Don Julian de San Chriftobal
El Maeftro Virgala Dominico
El Maeftro Ibaretta Benedictino

X 3

The

The abbot of St. Martin | The Marquis de la Hinojosa
Don Juan de la Rosa |
The Vicar of Toledo Santa Maria | Don Juan Valcarcel Canario
Father Cardenas a Capuchin | Don Antonio Angosto Colonel
El Maeftro Magin Mercenarian | With other perfons of diftinction to the
Another Maeftro of the fame order | number of forty.

" The accufed made his appearance in a yellow robe with a green taper in his hand, and was ordered to fit on a bench oppofite to the inquifitors, who had a table before them, covered with the papers relating to the procefs. One of the fecretaries began to read a fummary of the caufe which was followed by other papers, and continued till noon; at which time they had gone through the whole,

whole, having begun at eight in the
morning.

"The depositions of the prisoner were
read, taken after his confinement in
the prisons of the holy office; in which
he divided his life into three epochas.
The first comprehends the space of
thirty years, in Lima, and in Spain;
with respect to his notions, in which
though weak and a sinner, he confes-
ses his true and solid sentiments concerning religion, articles of faith,
dogmas, rites, and customs of the
church; as well as want of that improvement he afterwards acquired in
the second period. This includes
the space from his tour into foreign
parts, where losing his temporal felicity, and jealous of that of others in

 Spain,

Spain, he formed to himfelf his new maxims; acquired much knowledge in every branch of fcience, became acquainted with Voltaire and Rouf-feau, and other free-thinkers, whom he argued with, to fee if they could convince him : thus ftifling the qualms of his own confcience, he gave him-felf up to his opinions and plea-fures. The third period includes, from the year 1767, down to the pre-fent time, when full of pre-occupa-tions, and falfe ideas of the abufes of the regular and fecular clergy; his at-tention to population; his falfe no-tions of the prerogative, caufing impediments to the happinefs of ftates; the fetters of religion; and opi-nions of the Romans; he gave up his whole thoughts to the fettling new

colonies

colonies in the Sierra Morena ; and taken up with his own ideas, he fpoke without reflection, with temerity, with imprudence, urged on by his opponents, concerning the fallibility of the pope, the tribunal of the inquifition, and of all thofe things which in his opinion might retard or impede his projects : protefting that all, that had been faid and reported, had been ftrained into a different fenfe by his hearers, and others, who might have been fcandalized thereat.

" Thefe declarations were followed by the depofitions of feventy-eight witneffes, who certify feparately and jointly all the novelties, we find diffeminated amongft the free-thinkers

of

of the times; diſtinguiſhing particular caſes and of facts, blaſphemies *nominatim* maintained, and practical caſes on all theſe points. Many are confeſſed, and others he denies, ſaying he does not remember them, others that they were merely delivered in the names of their authors, inſiſting that he never believed them in his heart. That many were ſaid in a jocoſe manner, to try the temper of his hearers, and that he ſuffered himſelf to be carried away with the vain-glory of ſhining in converſation.—To the objections of having ſaid that St. Auſtin was a poor ſimple man, and that Peter Lombard, St. Thomas, and St. Bonaventure had retarded the progreſs of ſcience by their ſcholaſtic forms and abſtruſe manner, he

palliated

palliated, by saying, that in his opinion, if they had lived in these times, in which the mind has been so much improved by philosophy, they would have reaped greater profit, and when charged with his contempt of the most sacred mysteries, he retorts it upon the abuses of the clergy and hypocrites, on which head he spoke irreverently of confession and paschal communion.   In this manner he exculpates himself from a number of accusations, brought against him in the *Plenarium*, wherein 90 witnesses speak more fully and openly.

" He is moreover convicted by papers of his hand writing, as well as his own letters, which he has solemnly avowed; the spies and stratagems

have

have been difcovered by which, he endeavoured to perfuade the witnef-fes, to recede from their firft depofitions; alfo his intercepting and opening the letters of the inquifition and falfe anfwers given to hide his fecrets and intentions; the confidents employed in thefe acts, and the inftructions given by means of thefe thefts, and other arts, by which he difcovered all the proceedings of the inquifition, and their defigns; in a word, every method which human invention could devife to overfet the proceedings,

" That *the Roman Emperors were better than many holy kings*, he explains merely with refpect to natural virtues. That he ridiculed the religious

ous men of the order of St. Peter of Alcantara when in Rome, who prefenting themfelves to him on viewing the *Capitol*, he confeffes, acknowledging that their poverty and nakednefs cooled his enthufiafm in their favour. Of this kind there are an infinity of inftances throwing a ridicule on the moft facred fubjects. He calls the inftitution of the Carthufians *barbarous*, and if he preferred the ftate of matrimony to celibacy and fpoke with contempt of the religious vows of an afcetic life, and of continency, it was only to enconrage propagation in a holy manner, being fo much wanted in Spain: that all he had faid, and done, in the new fettlements, was to correct the abufe of alms, to encourage labour, and to

banifh

banish idleness, to which the settlers were prone, under pretence of going to mass, and other devotions in the churches. For his indecent pictures, and his portrait, holding a picture of Venus and Cupid, he lays the blame on the painters of Geneva, who did them without any orders from him. The enthusiasm of Crusades and the increpations of St. Bernard, who encouraged them so strongly; attributing the sales made by the faithful of their estates, with hopes of acquiring better in the holy land, *to the intrigues of the clergy, to get possession of them,* he represents, as merely discourse held in the name of those, who asserted such blasphemies in their writings: and the same excuse is given by him, when he

is

is convicted of having characterised
the order of St. Francis with ignorance, for securing a livelihood at
the expence of the public by repre-
senting poverty as honourable. . In
a word, all that St Evremont de-
claimed against the institutes of
Regulars; with what was published
before the councils of Constance and
of Trent, and the subtilities of the
present times, under a pretext of the
public good, and the advantage of
the subject; all this, is comprised
under different heads in this suit.
All that we hear from the literati of
the present age, the writings of free
thinkers, and what these oracles an-
nounce, as proceeding from prepos-
sessions, touching the jurisdiction
in no wise coercive of the church;

all

all thefe are, proved in the procefs ;
many are confeffed and many ill ex-
cufed, which are infinite in number ;
and time would be wanting, were I
to name many other circumftances
of this kind.   They are more than
fufficient to pronounce him a *formal
heretic*, to confifcate all his eftates,
declare him incapable of all honours
and dignities; to be banifhed from
the court, royal feats, new colonies,
Lima, and Seville 20 leagues round.
To be fhut up eight years in a convent, where he is to read *The fymbol of
faith* of Father Luis de Granada, and
The incredulous without excufe, of Father
Seneri, with other lefs penalties, and
to confefs his fins once a month.
The inquifitor general pardons him

from

from the *fambenito* (a), and he appeared in public without his crofs of knight-hood of the order of St. James.

(a) The *fambenito*, fays a Spanifh writer, is a gar-ment covering the breaft and fhoulders and wore by a reconciled penitent at his trial before the inqui-fitors. The name is an abbreviation of the words *faco benedicto* "bleffed garment." In the primitive church penitents were clothed in robes bleffed by the bifhop or prieft, and they ftood with them at the door of the church till they had performed their penances, were abfolved from their fins and admitted again into the bofom of the church ; which cuftom has been imitated by the inquifition, info-much that, though in the eyes of the world it is ig-nominious and affronting ; if thofe that wear it, continues the fame profound writer! accept with pa-tience, what may be faid of them by the vulgar, it may be of great merit in the fight of God.———
Tefero de la Lengua Caftellana, por " *Don Sabaftian de Cobarruvias Orozco capellan de Su Mageftad confultor del Santo Oficio de la inquificion.* Madrid, 1611

Y

On

"On hearing the fentence and find-ing himfelf declared *a formal heretic*, he faid, *not fo*, and fell from the bench like one in a fit: he made a folemn abjuration, after a protefta-tion of faith, was abfolved from cenfures, with all the formalities of the facred canons, and became the greateft object of compaffion. He de-clared in writing, that the utmoft ri-gour was nothing when compared to his wickednefs, and all appearances feem to befpeak repentance, but *de occultis non judicat ecclefia!*"

THE END.